Leading from the Middle: Teachers and Coaches

Mitchell Boling

Cover Design by Michael Gibson Graphics

ISBN: 979-8-70938-686-0

LEADING
FROM THE
MIDDLE:
Teachers and Coaches

~~~

MITCHELL BOLING

For teachers and coaches everywhere.
Thank you for what you do.

Contents

Introduction 1

Training by Firehose 7

Football is Leadership.. 25

Reluctant Learners.. 41

One-On-One Time 51

Five Traits of a Leader in the Middle 59

The GAS Factor 71

Leadership Theories.. 81

The Deep Dive 93

A Dogfight with Grover 101

Testimonials 109

Conclusion.. 119

About the Author... 123

Other Books by the Author.................................... 125

Introduction

Teaching is the highest art; before the doctor, there was a teacher. — Steve Perry

The worldwide COVID-19 pandemic of 2020 has adversely affected nearly every person in the world. Our daily habits have changed, in the name of social distancing and mask wearing. Everyone has tried to do their part in curbing the virus that has wreaked so much havoc in our society today. It affected not only how we conduct our daily lives; it also has affected us professionally on many levels. One that has been adversely affected is the teaching profession.

Due to the lockdowns and social distancing, the education of our children was forced to revert to the home for a while. Parents were then forced to conduct their children's education in place of their teachers. This created many hardships on families, due to the disruption of the norm. Parents had to pick up where the teachers had left off. Difficult changes at home had to take place, as homeschooling can be incredibly difficult, especially if the parents are not prepared to take on the task of teaching. To compound the situation further, some parents may have had to take leaves of absence from their professions, simply to afford the time to conduct the homeschooling.

What was discovered in many cases was that teachers (and coaches too) had been taken for granted. Teaching is difficult! What makes it more difficult is being unprepared for it, and yet still needing to perform the task for their children. We have always simply dropped our kids off at the school and trusted the teachers to show them the way. This also holds true for nearly every level of instruction, from high school, through college and beyond. Teachers are trusted to deliver the instruction, allowing students to grow intellectually or professionally. But if the teachers are no longer available, the situation becomes intensified. This discovery realized that the teaching profession has gained a lot of newfound respect, thanks to what they do.

Anyone can be a teacher, but not everyone has the internal fortitude and drive to make a career of it. It takes a special person to be a teacher or coach, someone who not only has the yearning to make a difference in the lives of others but also has the aptitude to become a leader. What was realized because of this pandemic was that teachers and coaches are leaders, plain and simple. To be a leader is to have the ability to influence people to go in the same direction. This aptly describes the teaching profession. Teachers and coaches want their pupils to go in the same direction toward the shared goal of education. They accomplish this through leadership.

The leadership they convey is something that I refer to as leading from the middle. Leading from the middle means that the leader is not at the top of his or her organization. Rather, they are found at every level of it. Teachers are right there in the trenches with their pupils. They are the leaders in their classroom, guiding the students on their journey. This is what leading from the middle looks like.

I am writing this book as an homage to teachers and coaches everywhere! I understand that what they do is special. They make daily sacrifices to teach our children and to show them the way. It is the same with coaches and adult educators. Teachers and coaches are leaders, for sure, and should hold a lofty standing in our society. But as I stated earlier, they are sometimes taken for granted, and not held on any sort of pedestal. It is for this reason that I am honoring them here, as the leaders I know they are. To begin, read these definitions as they relate to leadership.

Merriam Webster defines these three following terms found in the realm of leadership. Understand how they compare and complement each other:

Coach: to train intensively (as by instruction and demonstration)
Teach: to instruct by precept, example, or experience
Lead: to guide someone or something along a way

Looking through each definition, one should easily be able to understand that the three terms are very comparable to one another. The terms complement each other too. Coaching and teaching will always go hand in hand, but when we add the leadership definition, we can see that all three can be complementary. This is because teaching and coaching may also be described as 'guiding someone along a way.' Therefore, these definitions affirm my assertion that they can be used synonymously. What makes this important is how we use each concept in practice, in our daily lives. This also applies to those of us who are not teachers but instruct others in their daily work.

As a leader in the middle of an organization, we should practice each of these concepts as we go about our day. For example, I could take a new employee out on a task and coach him or her through it. I would demonstrate how to perform the task and then evaluate their completion. I could also teach new skills or procedures to an entire group of coworkers in a classroom-like setting. Doing something like this is very common in companies today, especially when new processes or procedures are published that need to be taught to the workforce. After learning the procedures myself, I would then be able to use my experience to instruct the coworkers in the new processes.

Throughout the book, I will present stories, concepts, and lessons on leading from the middle, with a lean toward teaching and coaching. Based on my experiences, the book will feature stories from my time working with the military, my love of football, and of course, leadership in business. What I hope is gained from this is that we can all utilize these concepts in our daily work lives, even if we are not professional teachers. Leaders are found everywhere within an organization, and as leaders, it is up to us to teach or coach our followers on processes and procedures found within our profession.

One of the methods I used while constructing this book was to create a survey for teachers and coaches to complete. It was very successful and returned a plethora of great insights into the makeup of teachers and coaches everywhere. Here are the questions that made up the survey:

Do you consider yourself a leader?

What leadership traits or characteristics would you say a person must have to become a great teacher or coach?

How much time do you typically spend in professional one-on-one interactions with your students or players?

Outside of your normal workday, how many additional hours do you typically spend per day performing activities for your class or team?

How much of your own money would you estimate that you spent on school supplies in one year?

The responses from this survey were very helpful, especially the first question which by the way, received a one hundred percent response of "Yes," as expected. These responses assisted me in writing chapters about the leadership of football coaches and players, the difficulties found in teaching reluctant learners, and the importance of one-on-one teacher/student time.

Then, some deeper leadership assumptions, with chapters discussing five traits of a leader in the middle and caring for our followers using an acronym (to be explained later) called GAS. This is followed by a discussion about four key leadership theories that describe teaching and coaching thought processes and behaviors.

After that, a chapter where digging into one's own pocket is necessary, just to be able to provide adequate instruction. This chapter discusses managers in non-teaching professions as well. Next, a short story about the time I received some real instruction from a seasoned fighter pilot, and how he schooled me in the art of aerial combat—a hint, it wasn't pretty.

The final chapter is probably the best one of all because, in this chapter, you will read about how the COVID-19 pandemic has altered teachers' leadership and teaching styles. I think we can all agree that every teacher and student in America has been affected by the pandemic regarding the new restrictions put into place to ensure their safety. This is a chapter that features statements from real teachers who describe how they have coped with these trying times. These powerful testimonials show the resilience of some of our best and brightest minds. I believe that these folks, teachers and coaches, are to be placed on pedestals. I hope you'll agree after reading their stories. But we have to get there first, so let's get on with it, shall we?

As I said, you will find in this book that I write about some of my military experiences. This involved teaching aircraft maintainers or supporting those learning to fly U.S. Air Force F-16 fighter jets. But it must be said that this is not a book about the military and not a book about military tactics or operational procedures. While I do write about fighter jets, remember that this book is about teachers and coaches being leaders, which includes fighter aircraft instructor pilots. Since I do present two chapters involving flying fighter jets, it must also be said that at no time has any classified information been disclosed. The (hopefully entertaining) experiences in the aircraft simulator cockpits have been included to showcase these teacher-leaders by displaying what they do for our military every day.

Having said that, right out of the gate comes the first chapter, based on my experience working in the U.S. Air Force F-16 fighter pilot schoolhouse. This is where every new F-16 pilot begins his or her journey of becoming a fighter pilot. These young pilots are put through the wringer, as the curriculum is extremely challenging. Their instructors are absolute experts in their field and do an outstanding job teaching the students how to employ the F-16 Fighting Falcon in combat. The training is so strenuous that it is sometimes referred to as *Training by Firehose*.

Training by Firehose

The duty of the fighter pilot is to patrol his area of the sky, and shoot down any enemy fighters in that area. Anything else is rubbish. — Manfred von Richthofen

The two U.S. Air Force F-16 Fighting Falcon jet fighters floated in the sky in line abreast formation, side by side, a mile apart. Cruising at 350 knots at 18,000 feet of altitude, both pilots continuously scanned the surrounding area, looking for enemy fighters. Combat Air Patrol or CAP missions were a staple of every F-16 fighter pilot's repertoire, protecting their skies from any hostile aircraft that may approach. This mission, should it come to it, could involve Aerial Combat Maneuvering or ACM. Most folks know this as simply, *dogfighting*.

The mission involved two pilots from the 308th Fighter Squadron at Luke Air Force Base, Arizona. The flight lead, a captain who was also an instructor pilot or IP, was in command of their formation as call sign *Viper One*. His wingman, *Viper Two*, was a young lieutenant on his first CAP mission. The 'LT' was itching for some action but was understandably very nervous about it at the same time.

The weather was nice with no wind, a few cirrus clouds in the distance, and visibility of well over six miles. The two fighters continued their cruise with Viper One on the left and the wingman a mile off to his right side. The LT looked over to his left, admiring the F-16 lead aircraft. As he scanned behind it, he spotted an approaching aircraft. It was right behind his flight lead!

"Viper One, BREAK LEFT! Bogey on your six, one mile," he called excitedly over the radio. Viper One didn't vocally respond because he was already banking quickly, ninety degrees to his left and beginning a hard pull around the corner. Viper Two matched him, and each pilot began looking over his left shoulder and up through the top of his canopy, trying to keep an eyeball on the unidentified aircraft.

The bogey had jumped them, having caught the two aircraft unaware. To quickly evade any missiles and then defeat the intruder, each F-16 began dispensing countermeasure flares while performing a maximum g turn toward the oncoming aircraft.

"Viper One, tally, engaged," radioed the flight lead. He had become the 'Engaged Fighter' which meant that he was the one the bogey had chosen to target. He was now on the defensive. The bogey had matched his turn to the left and was beginning to chase him around the circle they were making in the sky.

Meanwhile, Viper Two was trying very hard to identify the threat, because he could not attempt a kill until it was positively identified as a hostile aircraft. Until he could positively identify it, all three aircraft would wrangle in the sky for position. But identifying it was only part of the equation: if it turned out to be an enemy, then he had to put himself into a position where he could take a valid shot at it. Craning his neck over his left shoulder, he as the 'Supporting Fighter,' began maneuvering his F-16 into a 'lag pursuit' position, where his aircraft's nose would point at the exhaust of the intruder aircraft.

As he maneuvered, the seeker head on his selected weapon, an AIM-9 Sidewinder Air-to-Air missile, came to life having detected the heat emanating from the exhaust of the bogey aircraft. This began a continuous whining, almost growling tone in his helmet. At the same time, the Fire Control Radar or FCR had automatically acquired the bogey and indicated this to him via an audible, "*Lock*" in a robotic female voice known to all F-16 pilots as 'Bitchin' Betty.'

The aircraft avionics presented a firing solution through a combiner glass called the Head-Up-Display or HUD, mounted on the forward console of the cockpit. The solution displayed on the HUD was an FCR-generated box around the target along with a superimposed, AIM-9-generated diamond. It was through this glass that the pilot had everything he needed, to see what was directly in front of his aircraft, lock on and employ weapons.

He strained to see the bogey, all the while ensuring his aircraft maintained its kinetic energy as he pulled through the turn. The higher the g load, the slower the aircraft would become. In an air-to-air engagement, this was a fine balance the pilot needed to master. He added more power as he felt the aircraft slow, and relaxed his pull on the side stick controller a touch. His adversary had slowed as well through its turn, and he was able to gain on it a little bit. Now he could almost get a confirmation as it grew larger in his HUD. Looking, straining, looking, until...*there it is!* Twin tails, two engines, and presenting a quick silhouette as it rolled, for him to easily make an identification.

"Viper Two, HOSTILE Fulcrum. FOX two!" The growling AIM-9 leaped off the F-16's right wingtip and corkscrewed toward its target trailing a white plume of smoke. It was over in less than two seconds. The MiG-29 exploded in a ball of fire and began a slow wingover roll towards the desert floor below. The doomed enemy pilot had become too fixated on his quarry, the lead F-16, to notice that the wingman had successfully lined up a kill shot on him.

"Viper Two, SPLASH, HOSTILE Fulcrum! Angels seventeen, left turn," the LT said excitedly over the radio.

"Viper, knock it off. Viper One, knock it off," replied the flight lead to the wingman's kill call.

"Viper Two, knock it off," said the wingman.

Both aircraft immediately became frozen in flight, hanging in their left-turning positions, the MiG-29 halting its fall into the desert. A short two seconds later and the MiG disappeared altogether, and both F-16s returned to their starting points, sitting still at 18,000 feet. The simulator dome that surrounded the cockpits flickered for a moment, as the computers and projectors realigned the outside world to its starting point of a clean, clear blue sky with more than six miles of visibility.

I had mouse-clicked the 'Reset' button on my simulator control console, which commanded both F-16s and my MiG-29 to return to their starting positions. Each F-16 was sitting one mile, line abreast, with my aircraft situated a mile behind the flight lead. 'My' MiG-29 was just that, mine, as I was its pilot for this simulated ACM mission. The MiG, or simply 'threat' as we called it, was a flight simulator in its own right, with similar flying characteristics of the two F-16 sims. The only difference between the two types of simulators was that each fighter pilot flew inside a complete replica F-16 cockpit, enveloped within an entire simulated outside world. Mine was nothing more than a sidestick controller, throttle, and a forty-six-inch computer monitor which showed a cartoon depiction of a HUD and the F-16 targets.

To fly it accurately, I tracked the action and maneuvering of the three aircraft via a 'God's eye view' looking down on the entire battlefield. It was a large map of the area that was projected onto a giant screen in the front of the control room, which displayed a two-dimensional view of the three aircraft icons as they moved across the map during the simulation. The F-16s were blue, and my icon was red. I had to pay attention to how the three aircraft interacted on the God's eye, as well as looking at them through my own HUD. My role in this exercise was to target one of the F-16s, and simply follow it in a circle.

I was able to participate in this as a non-pilot because I did just that; fly around in a circle and become a 'duck' for the LT to kill. The LT was a student in the U.S. Air Force's F-16 Basic Qualification Course, often referred to as the 'B-Course.' The B-Course is where every USAF F-16 pilot begins his or her journey in the F-16. The course is conducted at Luke AFB, Arizona, and Holloman AFB, New Mexico. It lasts about nine months and involves lectures, simulator sorties, and actual flying. The students start at the very beginning, learning how to safely fly the F-16 and respond to in-flight emergencies, and then continue with learning how to employ the aircraft in combat. This involves Air-to-Air and Air-to-Ground missions, along with numerous other types of missions which involve large formations from four aircraft to a dozen or more.

The B-Course students are put through the wringer; often referred to as *training by firehose.* Training by firehose meant that they received a lot of information in a short period, sort of like having a firehose of information directed right at their face and turned on, full blast. As they progressed through each phase of the training, they practiced in the air what they learned in the classroom and simulator. For instance, after successfully completing the simulated ACM mission in our example, the LT will fly the same mission, sans live missiles, in an F-16 over the range in Arizona.

On it goes, until graduation day and then they're off to their first assignment as an F-16 fighter pilot. It is there, at their new base, where they will continue to fly and train on an ongoing basis and be ready to be called upon in a wartime situation. These young lieutenants and captains are truly some of America's greatest pilots who put their lives on the line daily, flying a Ferrari in the sky, affectionately known as the *Viper.* But they have to get through the B-Course first.

"Two, you were a little late on the kill that time," said Viper One over the intercom from his frozen cockpit.

"Yes, sir," the student replied.

"You need to make sure you're managing your energy properly, while still keeping your lift vector on the target. Chuckie, do you have anything to add?"

Travis 'Chuckie' Byrom was the Contract Instructor Pilot or CIP sitting next to me at the simulator console inside the darkened control room. A long-time fighter pilot, Chuckie had thousands of hours in the F-16 cockpit. Retired from the U.S. Air Force, he was now employed by a Department of Defense contractor to provide instruction to the students in the B-Course. He gave lectures, instructed during simulator missions, and even flew in the simulator with the students as their flight lead. The Air Force put a large amount of trust into the CIPs, knowing fully well that these retired fighter pilots provided the best training possible for their fledgling student pilots.

"Well, the only thing I have to add is that you could have killed the target more quickly if you already had your AIM-120 called up," he said with a South Texas drawl. "Based on your distance, you know you're in range for the AMRAAM, so as soon as you heard Betty confirm your radar lock, you could fire much more quickly than trying to mess with your AIM-9. Does that make sense?"

"Yes, sir," replied the LT.

"That's all I've got for now, One."

"Okay, then let's press on with the next setup. Console, we will do setup number four this time," said the flight lead.

"Copy, give me a sec," I replied. As 'Console' not only did I fly the threat, but I also controlled the scenario. A quick look at my setup sheet, a couple of clicks of the mouse button, and I was ready. "Console ready."

"Viper One, ready."

"Viper Two, ready."

"Viper, fight's on," said the flight lead.

With a click of the mouse, the three of us were flying once again. This time, my aircraft was positioned behind Viper Two as Chuckie watched the scenario unfold on the big screen at the front of the room. On this large screen were three important displays from inside each cockpit; two Multi-Function Displays or MFDs, and the HUD. The MFDs presented radar and navigation information, while the HUD showed airspeed, altitude, attitude, and firing solutions (among many other bits of important information) from the pilot's eye perspective. These images were blasted up onto the wall via an overhead projector, and the video was being recorded for later viewing in the post-mission debriefing session. This allowed the CIPs to observe what was occurring during the fight, which enabled them to make comments and suggestions as needed.

"Viper Two, BREAK RIGHT! Bogey on your six, one mile," called the flight lead.

Both Vipers quickly rolled ninety degrees to the right and began a hard pull through the turn, punching out flare decoys while they attempted to acquire the bogey.

"Viper Two, tally bogey, engaged," replied the wingman as he was pulling through the turn.

I continued flying straight on course for a five-count and then maneuvered away with a quick roll and turn to the left, then leveled out, pointed directly at Viper One. We were now headed 'beak to beak,' in fighter parlance, only seconds from a merge.

"Bogey SWITCHED! Engaged. Viper One engaged," radioed the flight lead excitedly.

"Viper One, continue," replied the wingman. Viper Two had now become the supporting fighter since I switched my attack over to his flight lead. This meant that he was no longer on the defensive and now must take the offensive while the flight lead and I tangled.

Now headed directly at one another at more than eight hundred knots closure, a split-second decision had to be made. At the merge, should I turn left, or right? The merge was where two opposing fighters met up in the sky as they flew past one another. I maneuvered slightly so that our right wings would be pointed at each other as we passed by. Upon merging with the F-16, I rolled right and stayed on a knife-edge for about one second, right wing pointing at the ground. The F-16 mirrored my action, and as we flashed by, it seemed our canopies would touch.

"Viper One, HOSTILE Fulcrum, engaged!" the flight lead practically yelled over his radio.

"Viper Two copies, maneuvering," came the wingman's reply.

The instant we went past each other, we both pulled into right turns across each other's tail at maximum g. By making this maneuver, we had entered into a two-circle fight, where each fighter began making its circle in the sky and at the end of each circle, another merge would take place. At each merge, the pilots must decide which way to turn. Depending on which way they turn, will either continue the two-circle fight or transition into a one-circle fight. A one-circle fight is one where both fighters are flying within the same circle. Our fight continued with a mirrored turn at each merge, resulting in a continuous two-circle fight much like the knights of yore, competing in a jousting tournament.

Because I had turned to the right, my momentum took me back toward Viper Two, thus crowding him as he maneuvered for a shot. Too close, and ignoring him anyway, I continued my right turn to head back to a merge with Viper One. At this point in the scenario, my only goal was to fly in a two-circle fight with Viper One, while waiting for Viper Two to kill me. Seems easy, right? Not so fast. By performing the late switch on the

14

initial attack, I gummed up all of Viper Two's shot geometry. He had to start over.

While Viper Two was attempting to target me once again, it was time for another merge with the flight lead. Again flashing by, canopy to canopy, we turned across each other's tail. On it went, our two-circle fight, a stalemate that lost hundreds of feet of altitude with every merge/circle. The 10,000-foot floor was getting close now, and the fight would have to be ended soon. If only Viper Two could kill me!

Chuckie was watching the action silently, concentrating on Viper Two's HUD data. His airspeed had dropped too low, his energy rapidly dissipated with every turn as he desperately tried to target my aircraft. Chuckie began to frown, heaved a heavy sigh, and finally threw his pen down in disgust onto the table in front of him. "Come on, kid!" he barked at the screen.

The fight continued toward the floor. Viper One and I had at least four merges, and Viper Two struggled with each one, as the supporting fighter. At one point, Chuckie and I looked at each other, to which I just shrugged my shoulders. And then he had an idea.

"Mitch, kill that son of a bitch!" said Chuckie, eyes blazing.

"Huh? You seriously want me to kill him?" As the console operator and not a rated fighter pilot, I was not supposed to interact with their lesson, other than to just target an aircraft and fly around in a circle. I was supposed to be a sitting duck for the students to kill. But this student was having a very difficult time with it, and Chuckie wanted to teach him a lesson, literally.

"YES! Kill him! He needs to know what can happen if he cannot get the shot off!"

"Okay," I said through a giant grin. I immediately broke off from Viper One and pointed my nose at Viper Two.

15

"HOSTILE SWITCHED! He's leaning on you, Two!" came the frantic radio call from the flight lead.

"Viper Two, tally HOSTILE Fulcrum, engaged," replied Viper Two as he started worrying about what to do next.

I quickly achieved a firing solution and let a missile go. On the God's eye view, a red missile icon appeared from my aircraft and tracked its way toward my new prey.

"VIPER TWO DEFENSIVE! SPIKED," yelled the LT over his radio as he attempted a hard left turn while punching out flares. But the missile hit home, and Viper Two's F-16 exploded right in front of me. Smiling, I could not resist performing a victory roll as I passed over his flaming F-16.

Inside his simulator cockpit, Viper Two's outside world began flashing, alternating quickly between red, blue sky, red, blue sky, red, for several seconds as his aircraft tumbled from the simulated sky. The red flashing symbolized his death and was meant to drive the point home for the student.

"Viper, knock it off, Viper One, knock it off," said the flight lead.

"Viper Two, knock it off," the student replied in a defeated tone.

I clicked the reset button on the console and all three aircraft returned to their starting points.

"Okay, Two, let's talk about this one, shall we?" Chuckie began.

"Yes sir," came Two's reply.

"First of all, let me ask you this: why was it that you couldn't target the hostile Fulcrum after One ID'd it? Were you not ready for a possible switch?" Chuckie posed.

"Yes sir, I was taken a little by surprise when the bogey switched to the lead. I guess I wasn't ready to assume the supporting fighter duties so quickly after I was the engaged fighter," the LT answered.

"Okay, so you weren't ready. Is that what I heard you say? You were surprised?" Chuckie replied flatly. "Did you not have your avionics ready, or were you still trying to work out the comm issues?" One of the key elements of learning to become a fighter pilot was learning the proper usage of the numerous statements and commands during a fight. Bogey, hostile, supporting, engaged, fox, etcetera. Fighter pilot lingo is like an entirely different language, and it takes a lot of skill and practice to learn. What makes it so difficult is trying to practice it while enduring the speed and mental pressure of an aerial dogfight such as this. Getting the communication right was just as important as achieving a firing solution on an adversary.

"I think I was stifled by the comm. I had my avionics set up, but the bogey switching took me by surprise."

"Okay," Chuckie said. "Now let's say there were no comm issues. Don't even think about what you have to say on the radio in this instance. Just tell me how you would maneuver to achieve a position where you can take a valid shot. What would you do?"

"Well, I would need to roll back in once I realized he was no longer targeting me, get my nose up so the radar can pick him up…but when he turned my direction after their merge, I just got all messed up. He was too close for me to do anything."

"Exactly. He was too close," Chuckie agreed. "…and then after the following merge, you still couldn't lock him." Chuckie continued, "Did you notice how each merge made things even worse for you to get a solution?"

"Yes sir…" the LT just tailed off his answer in defeat.

"Okay, okay," Chuckie said softly through his headset microphone, nodding while looking up at Viper Two's HUD video that was projected up on the screen. "So. Here's what you should have done." Chuckie closed his eyes for a moment, gathered his thoughts, and when he opened his eyes to continue, he took a different tone of voice that was a little more forceful. Not condemning or condescending; it was more of a serious, 'it's time to listen to me now,' tone.

"First of all," he said in his South Texas drawl, "the instant the flight lead called the bogey hostile, you should have been ready to fire. Once he ID'd the bogey as a hostile enemy, you should have had the shot off within two seconds, as long as One was safely out of the way. But you didn't, because you weren't ready, and you were *surprised* by how close the MiG got to you after the merge." He continued, "If you couldn't get the shot off, you needed to *immediately* get out of the way so that you could reengage. You had said that he got too close. Yes, that is going to happen. What you should do in a case like that is to get away. Now how do you get away?" he asked rhetorically, before continuing. "You need to extend away from the fight to give yourself enough room to maneuver for a timely follow-on shot attempt. Do you understand when I say you need to extend?"

"Yes sir, I need to maneuver so that I can get some distance to allow me a little more time to get the shot set up," the LT replied.

"Yes, that is right. You can maneuver laterally, vertically, or both to build the room you need. As you do so, you should continue to observe the bandit and use your observation to predict over time so you can get into position." Chuckie paused for a moment to allow his comments to sink in, and then continued. "What I would have done in your situation is extend laterally to the east, descending slightly while in full afterburner to preserve energy. Then as the bandit continued his turn, time my turn back in so that I can take my shot across the circle. All while making sure I'm not going to run into Number One. And remember, One is fixing to get shot down by this guy, so you'd better hurry back, right?"

"Yes sir."

"By extending away momentarily, you have given yourself a better geometry to make the shot. Does that make sense?"

"Yes sir," came the LT's reply, sounding a little more confident as he began to understand how to proceed.

"Okay then. One, do you have anything you'd like to add?"

"Nope. You said it all, Chuckie," replied the flight lead.

"Okay, then One, if you're ready, shall we press on?" said Chuckie.

"You bet. Console, let's do that one again," came the response.

"Console copies, ready," I replied while smiling over at Chuckie. He just looked back at me and shook his head, silently.

"Viper One, ready," said the flight lead.

"Viper Two, ready," responded the student.

"Viper, fights on," said the flight lead.

I clicked the button and the aircraft began flying, once again.

Learning how to become a fighter pilot is most definitely, training by firehose. These pilots have heaps of information thrown at them, and they must catch and retain as much of it as possible to become successful in their quest to fly the finest fighter aircraft in the U.S. Air Force. Instructors like Chuckie help to make this happen. His teaching method during that simulator mission exemplified the expertise required to bring these students along in their training.

When Chuckie told me to kill the student, he did so because he wanted the student to experience what could happen if he made a mistake. Mistakes in fighter aircraft lead to pilots getting killed. So, his example of being shot down himself had driven home the point of what could happen if he messed up. He could die. Chuckie had successfully displayed to the student this aspect of being a fighter pilot.

I also enjoyed listening to Chuckie as he spoke to the student following his mistake. Chuckie had a reputation of being a no-nonsense guy, someone who knew exactly what he wanted to say and didn't have a problem saying it. Sometimes, his methods rubbed people the wrong way, but he always seemed to have a purpose. His purpose in this example was to get the message across in the appropriate manner so the student would learn from it. But his stern suggestions on how he should have maneuvered weren't what influenced the student to learn. What made the student learn was how Chuckie handled the lead-up to the stern talk. Chuckie posed the correct questions to him in a soft, easygoing manner. He empathized with the student's frustrations and had employed a keen listening skill to the student's explanation of his errors. He then explained in no uncertain terms, what the student needed to do to be successful. Chuckie's handling of that ACM engagement helped the student to realize his errors, learn from them, and move forward.

This experience also settled in my mind that Chuckie was one of the best instructors I had ever seen, fighter pilot or not. His way of handling the instruction seemed so out of character for him, based on what I had seen outside of the classroom, that it took me a little bit by surprise. In short, I was impressed.

I was impressed not because it seemed out of character, rather because his method was exactly what was needed in that situation. The process of becoming a fighter pilot is very intense. In my experience, fighter pilots are very direct people. They must be because theirs is an extremely dangerous business. Thus, their teaching methods must be direct as well. During every fighter sortie, simulated or actual, a lesson is learned. And after their mission has ended, the instructor and student relive what they had just completed in what is called a debriefing session.

In debrief, every aspect of their flight is recounted to a tee. The instructor uses two 'sticks,' which are small wooden F-16 replicas on two-foot-long dowels, during his debrief of the mission. These visual aids represent his and his wingman's aircraft during their flight and are a great way of helping to explain the maneuvering characteristics or relative positions of the aircraft during their flight. Inside the debriefing room is also where the knives come out. In a critical training session like a B-Course mission, it is a one-sided knife fight. It is like this because the IP must be brutally honest with his student. All fighter pilots must have this quality if they are to be successful. As I said, their business is very dangerous. It is because of this, that they must confront every mistake to ensure it does not reoccur. It is the nature of their business and people will die if they fail to do their job correctly.

So, yes, Chuckie's methods were appropriate to the teaching lesson. But not every profession needs to be this intense. When I was an instructor in the U.S. Air Force, I taught aircraft maintainers the intricacies of the F-16 integrated avionics suite. My course was three months long and included sessions from the podium, maintenance trainer, and actual aircraft. The students came out of the course being very familiar with the theory, troubleshooting methods, and operational characteristics of a dozen unique avionics systems. But I didn't employ the same teaching methods as Chuckie, because it wasn't the same dynamic. Sure, people can be killed in aircraft maintenance and I did talk about this in my course. But the focus in my course was that the students needed to come away with confidence on how the systems worked and how to operate and troubleshoot them.

The methodology used in my course was probably like most technical schools. I provided lectures, critical reading, and practical exercises. I demonstrated how to perform a task and then graded the students on how they performed the same task. No firehoses here; my teaching sessions were not performed at 800 knots of closure, rather a slowed down approach that most teachers are familiar with. So, it was a different dynamic than teaching someone how to become a fighter pilot. Still effective, just a different dynamic.

Being a teacher is like being a coach. Regarding the fighter pilot, I think 'coach' is a very apt word to use. Maybe a football coach would be even more appropriate. The coach is going to sit a player down and tell him directly, how his mistakes affected the team and its success in winning a game. He will tell him directly and then say to "Do it again," just as the IP said during the ACM training mission. This makes sense, and for most people, the coach is considered the leader of their team. Since we can correlate coaching with teaching, I think it also makes sense that teachers are leaders, too.

When we teach someone how to do something, we are leading them toward a goal. The goal in teaching is to help a student understand the content. It is the same with leadership. We want to influence those who follow us to go our way, to travel toward a shared goal. So, yes, teachers are leaders in this sense. Most people would agree with this, as the teacher-student relationship could be seen as a leader-follower relationship. But this doesn't have to be in the formal sense, as in a schoolhouse setting. Teachers, coaches, and leaders are found everywhere in our society, up and down the spectrum. Let me explain.

While we might equate teaching and coaching as formal leader-follower relationships, we also must look at a more informal relationship between the two. What I mean by this is that it can be found somewhere in the middle. Teaching/coaching/leading does not have to happen from the top down. It can happen anywhere within an organization. When an electronics technician takes a new employee out on a task to replace a computer system, he is leading the new employee through the process. He can coach him as he demonstrates the task, and lead him to completion. If the technician is certified to perform a task, he should be able to teach it, informally. We refer to this as on-the-job training or OJT.

Most companies understand that this is how their employees are trained. OJT is essential in the ongoing performance of tasks. Additionally, OJT is conducted by leaders in the middle. These trained experts pass on their knowledge to newcomers and lead them on the path to the shared goal. This is teaching, this is coaching, and this is leading. This is leading from the middle.

Many different methods of teaching/coaching/leading abound. Looking back to our example, training by firehose is an essential teaching methodology for those yearning to become fighter pilots. But this is not the case in most professions. Many professions teach through different methodologies, each tailored to the task at hand, or more specifically the lesson to be learned. But each methodology has the same basic traits in the process of teaching and learning. The teacher must be able to listen to the student. The teacher must also be able to articulate proper instruction to the student. Lastly, the teacher must be able to empathize with the student. If these basic traits sound familiar, it is because they are much of the same traits found in the realm of leadership. What this boils down to is this: teachers are leaders too.

Anyone can be a teacher or coach, the same as anyone can be a leader. They simply must demonstrate the knowledge, empathy, and care required to communicate information to their students, players, and followers alike. Leaders do not have to be at the top, because leaders are found everywhere. Leadership should not always be looked at as a top-down approach, but as an all-encompassing skill set that anyone can employ, no matter their level within a company. Referring to Chuckie in his role of teaching the fledgling pilot how to perform aerial combat: he wasn't at the top of the food chain in providing the lesson, rather he was in the middle. Chuckie was performing as a leader in the middle, with the rest of us.

Yes, teachers and coaches are leaders for sure. In this chapter, I said that an instructor pilot is very similar to a coach. This was because the coach will sit his player down and tell them straight up how they failed. A dose of tough love, if you will. Coaches are extremely passionate about their craft. They are certain to ensure their players learn from the lessons they are providing and do so by using numerous leadership types. The next chapter will touch on two types of leadership, legacy and medial. To do so, we will look at another of my passions, football. Because *Football is Leadership*.

Football is Leadership

You don't win with X's and O's. What you win with is people. – Joe Gibbs

I am a devout fan of the National Football League's Seattle Seahawks. I am definitely not a fan of the New England Patriots, however. I know, I know; how does this statement relate to a book about leadership? Please bear with me while I elaborate for a moment. You might understand why I made that statement if you knew the history between these two teams. Football fans might remember that the Seahawks had lost Super Bowl XLIX to the Patriots in a devastating fashion. But this one game does not tell the entire story. There is more to it, as these two teams have had a unique history over the years. The Seahawks' inaugural season in the National Football League was 1976. The team endured numerous disappointing seasons, as do most teams that are starting out. But the 1992 season was their worst by far, with a win-loss record of 2-14.

The 1992 season was very disappointing for the Seahawks and their fans, but owning the worst record comes with a perk. The team with this negative distinction is afforded the first pick in the following season's college player draft. As the season ended, the future looked bright for the Seahawks. A quarterback from Walla Walla, Washington named Drew Bledsoe had become a national star, breaking numerous quarterback records at Washington State University. He was sure to be the number one pick in the 1993 draft, and seemed to be just what the Seahawks needed; their hometown hero to come and lead the Seahawks to glory. But of course, it didn't work out that way, thanks to the New England Patriots.

In 1992, the Seahawks weren't the only disappointing team in the NFL. The New England Patriots shared this distinction with an identical 2-14 record. Because of this, a tiebreaker had to be decided. As fate would have it, one of the two games the Seahawks won that season was against the Patriots themselves. So, the Seahawks were just a little better than the Patriots that year. This awarded the first pick to the Patriots, who promptly made Drew Bledsoe the face of their franchise. The Seahawks selected quarterback Rick Mirer second, and from here the teams went in opposite directions.

Over the next four seasons, the Seahawks missed the playoffs, while the Patriots, led by Drew Bledsoe, were contenders every year, making it to Super Bowl XXXI where they lost to the Green Bay Packers. As Drew Bledsoe's run with the Patriots began to wane, another quarterback stepped into the spotlight. Three years after their trip to Super Bowl XXXI, and before the 2000 season, the Patriots drafted a little-known quarterback from the University of Michigan. His name was Tom Brady.

A supposed journeyman quarterback, Brady backed up Bledsoe during his rookie season. The next season another twist of fate occurred for the Patriots. In week two against the New York Jets, Drew Bledsoe sustained a serious chest injury which would sideline him for the rest of the season and ultimately end his time with the team after nine years. In stepped a wide-eyed Tom Brady, who nervously took the reins of his New England Patriots. The rest, as they say, is history. At the end of that season, Tom led his team to a victory in Super Bowl XXXVI over the St. Louis Rams, where he was named the Most Valuable Player of the game. He had successfully cemented his status as the new face of the franchise and unquestioned leader of his team.

As the new face of the franchise, Tom Brady has become the quintessential quarterback and consummate leader for the New England

Patriots. Over the next nineteen years as the Patriots' leader, the 'Future Hall of Famer' has won six Super Bowls (including the one over my Seahawks) and established numerous other records along the way. So, you might now understand why I am not a fan of the New England Patriots, going all the way back to 1992!

But that is not what this chapter is about (by the way, thanks for hanging with me while I explained the unique history between these two NFL teams). This chapter is about one of my passions, leadership. In this chapter, we will discuss two very important concepts: legacy leadership and medial leadership. After this, we will tie it all together and discuss who is responsible for creating these types of leaders in football as well as in life: Coaches.

Legacy Leadership

Legacy leadership can be characterized as a leader who inspires others to do their very best, in a manner that is seen by the followers in a revered way. The leader they follow is a celebrity in their field; not necessarily famous, but can certainly be the 'Face of the Franchise.' This doesn't mean the person has to be an actual celebrity. What it means is that the leader is the pinnacle leader in his or her organization. Sometimes the person can be famous, but most often the person is simply a higher-level employee or manager who the followers look up to with admiration.

This legacy leader may also be a teacher or a coach. Think about it. Teachers and coaches strive to leave lasting impressions on their pupils. Whether in the classroom or on the football field, teachers and coaches convey their information in such a manner that will enable the students and players to look up to them. In some cases, the pupils remember these lessons throughout their lifetime. If this occurs, then the teacher or coach has been successful in creating a legacy for themselves, in the eyes of their students and players. When the students and players begin to emulate the lessons they were taught, they have perpetuated the concept of legacy leadership.

We all remember people from our past who had helped or taught us in one way or another. These people are legacy leaders, as they left their impression on us. I remember my first Little League baseball coach, Mr. McCabe. He was a Riverside County Sheriff's Deputy who coached our team in Eagle Mountain, California in 1973. I remember as a ten-year-old boy, how I looked up to him and hung on every word as he taught me how to play the game. Often he, while still wearing his sheriff deputy uniform, would demonstrate how to field ground balls at second base. I still remember the lessons he taught me, and I still field ground balls the same way, more than forty years later! I taught my son how to play baseball using the same methods that Mr. McCabe had taught.

This man made such an impression on me that I idolized him. He was my leader on the baseball field. When our family relocated to Arizona the following year, he took the time to write me a letter, which I thought was awesome. In the letter he had asked how I was adjusting to my new environment, was I playing baseball, and most importantly, how my family was doing. He was just a good man, a leader in the Riverside County Sheriff's Department, whom I looked up to and missed very much at the time. The letter he wrote me was the first letter I had ever received that was not a birthday card. It was my very first letter, and I still have it today. I never saw him again, and sometimes wonder how his life panned out. I looked up to him as my coach, as he was my legacy leader.

> Legacy leadership is when people are inspired by who you are, not simply by what you do. — Scott Cochrane

This quote resonated with me, as I am one who emphatically believes in the different powers in the leadership continuum. The leadership power that sits at the top of all others is *referent power*. One with referent power is revered by his or her followers, as they usually exhibit a charisma or confidence that makes others comfortable in following them. They want to follow! The followers know that this leader will take them through difficult or demanding situations. Additionally, followers feel like they want to make their leader happy or model their own behavior after that of the leader.

This sounds very similar to the quote from Mr. Cochrane. As with my baseball story, legacy leadership is where the leader will leave something behind when he or she is gone. This is because the people who follow them are inspired by who they are, as leaders, and want to continue this behavior after the person has departed. This sounds like something that would be incredibly satisfying to anyone in a leadership position, having their followers pick up where they left off. Now, let's relate this to the NFL and the New England Patriots.

The New England Patriots have been a very successful organization for decades. They have built a winning team through hard work and the application of legacy leadership. Since drafting Drew Bledsoe in 1993, the Patriots have enjoyed twenty-two winning seasons and only four that were under the .500 mark. Let's look at some other numbers over the same time, comparing it to another team, the Cleveland Browns.

Since 1993, the Patriots have had eight starting quarterbacks; Bledsoe, Brady, and six others who only started because of injuries or planned rest for the two leaders. By contrast, the Browns started *thirty* quarterbacks. Additionally, twenty of their twenty-three seasons were losing ones. Now, I'm not here to bash on the Browns or their fans. I just wanted to use a couple of well-known statistics for the comparison. What I want to show, and what I want you to think about as you read the rest of this chapter, is how the Patriots organization's successes (or maybe the Browns' failures) measure up to your own organization's successes (or failures). The NFL is a business, and the Patriots are one of the 'companies' in this business. Why have they become so successful? Let's explore some possibilities.

This is because in part, of the leadership qualities that their owner, coaches, and players have exhibited over the years. Just as in business, all levels of a company need to have the component of leadership to succeed. In football, the quarterback is the key leader on the field. The team will go as he goes, winner or otherwise. Therefore, all NFL teams are looking for that 'Face of the Franchise.' The Patriots just happened to strike gold twice in a row with their quarterbacks.

Drew Bledsoe was the leader of the team through the nineties, and they rallied around him to become a winner. When Tom Brady took over, he followed the example that Drew had left for him and continued his winning legacy. But as Tom matured as the starting quarterback and leader of his team, he took it to another level through his play and leadership qualities.

Tom Brady is a confident, highly motivated leader. As an NFL fan, I hate it when his team plays my team. Just looking at him whether he is in the huddle, on the sidelines, or holding the Lombardi Trophy over his head, he exudes confidence and leadership. In the huddle, he is confident. On the sidelines, he is intense (especially when the team is behind or someone had made a mistake). Holding the trophy, he is exuberant, knowing that he once again, was the lynchpin in leading his team to victory.

Legacy leadership. Tom Brady exemplifies this concept. I realized this as I watched their game against the New York Jets during the 2019 season. He threw a pass to rookie wide receiver Jakobi Meyers, who made a great, diving catch. Watching this, I immediately thought that this rookie will someday be telling his grandkids that he caught a pass from the Great Tom Brady, and the spark for this chapter was born in my mind.

Tom Brady will be leaving a legacy, one of leadership when he (finally) retires from the NFL. A Hall of Famer for sure, he has built his legacy by setting or breaking records and leading his team to seven Super Bowl titles (his latest after the 2020 season, playing for Tampa Bay). Players from many teams emulate him, respect him, and most importantly, learn from him. He has set the example of how to perform in arduous circumstances. He has been the consummate leader for his team and has the 'been there, done that' attitude. People in and out of football want to be like him.

This brings to mind the 'Be Like Mike' advertising campaign by Gatorade in the early 1990s. Like Tom Brady, Michael Jordan was the leader of his team, the Chicago Bulls. He led them to numerous NBA titles, and it was his referent power and legacy leadership that powered them through. Jordan's positive example and success led to people wanting to be like him, even to this day. People want to have someone to follow. People want to be like the charismatic leader they admire. It's the leader's legacy that contributes to this thought.

Remember that this is not about sports. It's about leadership. When I say that people want to be like a leader they admire, it's not all-inclusive to those on a sports team. People look for someone to follow in their own lives, at home and work. Think about how Tom Brady and the New England Patriots' organization relate to your organization. Is there a leader in your group who has the intensity, referent power, and legacy leadership that Tom Brady conveys? Is there someone in your organization who you yearn to follow or be like? What if this leader is you? Are you presenting the winning attitude that others want to match?

Legacy leadership is certainly a key thought in the realm of leading. As a follower, I would hope to become as successful as the leader I admire.

As a leader, I would hope that I am setting a positive example for my own followers. If an organization has a leader who can leave a lasting legacy of his or her leadership qualities, then that organization will become successful in the long run. Just like the New England Patriots.

Medial Leadership

As the face of the franchise, Tom Brady is an aggressive and devoted leader, demanding the best effort out of each player on the team. He did this while leading from the front, the key leader in his organization, the New England Patriots, and beginning in the 2020 season, the Tampa Bay Buccaneers. Every football team has a player like him, the face of the franchise and recognized leader in the locker room and on the field. But not all leaders are apparent; some of them exist in the background, working their magic from the middle of their organization. We will explore these medial leaders here.

> Medial leadership is when people lead from the middle of an organization, as opposed to from the top. – Mitchell Boling

The head coach of an NFL football team is its overall leader who leads from the top. Yes, the star player might be the face of the franchise, and the key leader out on the field, but the coach is in the position to make strategic and tactical decisions for the team. It is up to the head coach to set the tone on how the team will conduct its daily business. It is up to the head coach to provide the vision of where he wants the team to go. As the leader on the top, he cannot do this all by himself. He requires the help of some like-minded people in the middle.

These people in the middle make up his coaching staff. Every football team has numerous coaches that work together to help run the team. An NFL team is typically comprised of as many as twenty-five or more coaches on staff. The main ones are the offense, defense, and special teams. Others include sub-components to these main groups, such as linebackers' coach, quarterbacks' coach, running backs, receivers, linemen, and the list goes on. There will be a coach for every position on the team. These coaches are key to the success of the overall team. It is up to these medial leaders to set the tone within their groups so they will be able to gel together and achieve the desired effect, which is winning.

Once the sub-teams gel together and practice their own vision of how best to contribute, the rest of the team begins to excel as an overall group. It is these leaders, these coaches who make this happen. The coaches lead the players in the trenches toward victory. We can think about this in a business sense as well.

It is left to the leaders in the middle to make the organization go. Once the sub groups gel together, the overall group begins to enjoy success. It is similarly true in business. So, these football teams are not too different from the typical business models that are found everywhere in the economy. Running a football team is very similar to running a typical business. There must be an overall leader at the top, along with medial leaders throughout the center of the organization. While these sub-grouped coaches make up the brunt of the medial leadership, we must not forget the players have their leaders in the middle, too.

Every football team has its leader on the field; usually, it is the quarterback who controls the movement of the ball downfield. Sometimes we hear this player being referred to as coach on the field. Sounds like the quarterback should be the leader, right? Maybe, but it is not always so. We should be aware that the quarterback isn't always the key leader of the team. Other leaders abound in the middle of the team. First, let's look at the make-up of a football team itself.

In the NFL, each team has fifty-three players. Each player belongs to a smaller group of specialties that when working together, contribute to the success of the team. The three major team units are the offense, defense, and special teams. Within these elements are smaller subgroups, as referred to earlier. There are linemen, receivers, running backs, and quarterbacks on offense. On defense, there are linemen, linebackers, and defensive backs. Lastly on special teams will be linemen, kickers, and associated players who bring their unique attributes to the team. Many of these players also belong to the first-mentioned subgroups like receivers and backs.

Within each of these subgroups is a medial leader. The leader in each subgroup has taken the responsibility of ensuring each member of their group does their part. This leader might be more experienced than the other players, due to their length of time in the profession, or simply displays a higher talent level on the field. Either way, the players in the group gravitate to this leader, trusting in him to show them the way. These players lead by example, because they are out there on the field with their teammates, putting in the work. They provide the impetus to do well, based on their talk and their actions, leading by example. Leading by example is probably the most common tool in our leadership toolbox, and football players must practice this if they want to become successful. Let's look at two examples from two of 2019's NFL playoff teams.

The Baltimore Ravens began the 2019 playoffs as the number one seed in the AFC championship tournament. They accumulated a 14-2 record, the best in the NFL. Their leader on the field, quarterback Lamar Jackson, strikes me as a quiet leader, a rather shy player who does his best leading on the field. I see him as an introverted player with freaky good athletic ability. His play is what motivates followers from within his team. They know that he will take them to more wins and therefore, will do their part to help make that happen. But what about the other leaders, those in the subgroups? Let's take, for instance, offensive lineman Marshal Yanda.

Drafted by the Ravens in 2007, Yanda has become the leader of the team, a veteran who continuously plays at a high level. Not only is he the leader in the lineman's group, but the entire team looks up to him as their leader. He leads by example and often provides a motivational speech before heading out to the field. He has earned the respect of his teammates, who readily follow his lead and are ready to go out and win. But we don't always hear about people like Marshal. We see the leader on the field, usually the quarterback, making the plays and spurring his team to go forward. It is important to remember that leaders are found everywhere, including in those subgroups. Their influence can go beyond the walls of their small group and can inspire an overall organization's journey toward greatness. They are leading from the middle.

Speaking of the middle, how about the leadership of a middle linebacker? The Seattle Seahawks' middle linebacker is Bobby Wagner. He is the unquestioned leader of the defense, and one of the most respected players on the team. Again, we usually see the leader on the field as the quarterback, Russell Wilson. While Wilson's leadership is evident from early on in his career, the same can be said for Wagner. Drafted by the Seahawks in 2012, Bobby Wagner is the mainstay of their defense. One of only two remaining defensive players (KJ Wright) from their 2014 Super Bowl XLVIII winning team, Wagner has the experience, talent, and determination to lead his teammates to their goals. Not only is he the leader in the linebacker's room, but on the overall team as well. Wagner, along with Wilson and Neiko Thorpe, were voted by their teammates as the captains of their team. All NFL teams do this, as evidenced by the "C" displayed on the captain's uniform.

Leadership is more than a title. Meeting with officials for the coin toss is the easy part of being a captain. Everyone might see this role but your most important responsibility is keeping your teammates focused on a common goal when the coaches aren't around. – Jamy Bechler

Those who are elected to be the captain of their team have demonstrated the leadership required to make a difference on the field and off. Their teammates gravitate to them based on their leadership traits as well as their athletic abilities. Often, the captains are compared to their coaches. ESPN college football analyst Kirk Herbstreit stated during the November 7, 2020 telecast of Clemson vs Notre Dame, "Clemson quarterback Trevor Lawrence is like a coach on the field." What he meant was that Lawrence had become so familiar with the offense, that he had a command of the flow of the game. He could direct his players through setups and blocking schemes, based on his pre-snap read of the defense. He knew exactly what he wanted to do with the offense, and this confidence and ability helped to influence his teammates to follow him. Herbstreit was referring to Trevor Lawrence being their leader.

Trevor Lawrence was not the formal leader (coach) of the team, but he assumed the role of leader in the middle (coach on the field) through his play and leadership skills. But how did he become the coach on the field, the team's natural leader? It was due to the coaching staff, led by head coach Dabo Swinney. This is what coaching staffs do, prepare their players for the game by pushing them to bring out their best athletic abilities, as well as their leadership traits.

But coaches don't just prepare their players to be successful on the field. They also prepare them for life off the field. It is up to the coaching staff of every team in organized sports to prepare their players for life after sports. Coaching staffs teach and prepare people for leadership, plain and simple. The process of this is realized in the trenches on the field, with the leaders in the middle emerging to the forefront as captains of their teams.

> Football, to me, is just the unique opportunity to have a pathway into their lives. I want them to truly love their experience, and not just be a football player, but to grow and be a person of excellence that just happens to be a good football player, too. And my philosophy is: If we develop them that way, football will take care of itself because they create habits of excellence that carry over. - Dabo Swinney in an interview with David Hale of ESPN

Dabo Swinney has transformed the Clemson University football team into a powerhouse program that is feared and revered across the nation. He led the Tigers to the national championship game four times in five years, winning the championship twice. Part of this success is that his players have bought into what he was selling. Dabo is an outstanding leader, one who has all the traits to be successful. He is charismatic, empathetic, and energetic to name a few. His players love him, and he loves them right back. These traits and behaviors are important in the development of teams and players.

It should be podium-stomped here that Dabo isn't simply trying to win games. Based on his quote above, he is in the business of developing people to be their best. He is in the business of growing leaders. These leaders appear during their time playing football, but they ultimately become successful in their own lives long after the cheering fans fade away. He does this in part through the traditions he has established along the way. One of the traditions he instituted is called the 'Tiger Walk,' which takes place a couple of hours before each home game.

At the beginning of the Tiger Walk, busses carrying the football team pull up to the front of the stadium. The players leave the bus and begin a slow walk through the throngs of diehard Clemson fans a couple of hundred yards to the stadium entrance. The players aren't in uniform just yet; each wears a business suit, which demonstrates the serious nature of this pregame ritual. By wearing a suit, each player presents an air of business first, with focused intensity toward the task at hand. This is also part of being a leader, and Dabo Swinney has taken the responsibility for molding these young men into leaders during their time with the team as well as afterward.

So, football is about creating leaders! We can realize this through the different levels of leadership, from those down in the trenches to the obvious face of the franchise. Coaches push their players to be their very best, not only in their chosen sport but also in life in general. The players who learn this the quickest become those leaders in the middle. They become the 'coach on the field,' that every teammate looks up to, knowing they will lead them through adversity toward the shared goal of winning.

Leaders are found nearly everywhere on a football team. Whether it is someone like Tom Brady who practices legacy leadership by making people want to be just like him, or Marshall Yanda, who quietly practices medial leadership from the trenches of the offensive line. We cannot forget the elected captains of their respective teams, leaders like Russell Wilson, Bobby Wagner, or Trevor Lawrence. Leaders are found everywhere, and it is all due to the coaches who influenced these players to play and act their absolute best. This is all due to coaches like Bill Belichick, Pete Carroll, Dabo Swinney, and even Mr. McCabe. These men have had a direct influence on the lives of the players they led, and the players will never forget them for it.

For those who have played sports, think about your coaches for a minute. Think back and remember what they taught you. Remember how they taught you to swing a club, spike a volleyball or throw a strike. Think about what leadership behaviors they exhibited at the time. Did they provide honest feedback, were they energetic, did they rally the troops? Did any of it rub off on you? I'll bet it did. I'd be willing to bet that most people who played sports in their youth are demonstrating leadership behavior in their lives right now, which was learned from experiences with their coaches. You should thank them for it.

Now, think about this in your workplace, outside of sports. Who is the team captain of your group? Who in your workplace would you consider to be the leader? It might be the Senior Manager, the face of your franchise, who leads the entire team through vision and experience. It might also be your coworker, down in the weeds, punching out widgets on an assembly line. It might even be you! If so, then step up and take the responsibility to do your part. Because leading from the middle will reveal dividends down the road, personally and professionally. Leaders are made in the middle, as this is where the work happens. Just as in football, those of us on the line are just as important to the success of an organization as are those at the top.

Now that we have established the leadership tendencies of coaches, next we will look at a very important issue that teachers and coaches face every day. Right off the bat, we will talk about students who do not seem to be interested in learning. These folks could not care less what the teacher is trying to explain to them, and they become quite a challenge for the teacher. Teachers who have these types of students must utilize every bit of their leadership skills to eventually get through to them. I refer to these students in the next chapter as *Reluctant Learners*.

Reluctant Learners

I cannot teach anybody anything; I can only make them think. — Socrates

One of the most difficult challenges in teaching is when a teacher is faced with reluctant learners. A reluctant learner is only in the classroom because they were told they had to be there. They are not interested in the subject matter, nor are they interested in paying attention during instruction. This is a great challenge for the teacher because it is up to them to try and bring the student around and begin to listen and learn the content. It is up to them to try and make it interesting for the student. This can be very difficult, and unfortunately, it becomes very easy for the teacher to just give up and allow the student to continue behaving in that disinterested manner. Teachers who are leaders resist the temptation to let it go, and instead, try harder to bring the students into the fold.

It kind of sounds like leadership, right? Bringing someone into the fold, indeed. This is exactly what leaders do every day. The goal of leadership is to get everyone to go in the same direction, and continuing to practice this in the classroom is a sign of determination and leadership on the teacher's part. Teachers must become beacons for their students, and a big part of that is for them to always display the traits of a leader. Traits like patience, authenticity, empathy, and compassion come to mind. These traits were the top answers to a recent survey when asked what traits or characteristics a person must have to become a great teacher or coach.

When a teacher or coach displays these traits, they will undoubtedly become more in tune with their students. They will have a higher success rate in turning those who are reluctant into those who are interested and engaged with the subject matter. This will also lead to a student becoming more in tune or engaged with the teacher him or herself. If the student has a positive experience with the instruction, they are more apt to not only learn the subject matter but remember what their teacher did for them. Teachers and coaches become positive memories for their students for years to come. Heck, I still remember Mrs. Sneddon, my third-grade teacher.

The gist of this is to demonstrate that teachers already know they are leaders, but the students may not realize this (yet). Once the teacher/student relationship matures, a bond has been created. Therefore, teachers and coaches must practice the leadership traits and characteristics, so they can be there for their students and players.

Students, especially younger ones, may not realize that they are being exposed to leadership. So, it is up to the teacher or coach to provide that for them. You see, teachers and coaches do not only teach the subject matter. They also teach life lessons. This is true even with adult learners. When I was an instructor in the U.S. Air Force, I was required to weave the Air Force core values into every lesson plan.

U.S. Air Force Core Values
  Integrity first
  Service before self
  Excellence in all we do

As an aircraft maintenance instructor, it seemed to be a difficult task, weaving in these phrases while teaching how to work on aircraft. But once I got used to it, it became second nature. It also felt like it was not contrived or forced upon the students. The more I taught, the better I was at providing these thoughts. For instance, my simplified default lesson plan might have read like this:

1. Objective: Identify the facts and principles of the Fire Control Radar (FCR)
2. Identify the basic components of the FCR
3. Discuss facts and principles of the FCR
4. Discuss theory of operation of the FCR

This lesson plan outline would be an example of what to teach in an eight-hour time frame, as an introduction to FCR. How am I going to discuss this for eight hours? This is when the instructor's personalization comes into play. I was expected to personalize my lesson plan using my own experiences and knowledge of the subject matter, while also weaving in the Air Force core values. After doing so, my lesson plan might have read something like this:

1. Objective: Identify the facts and principles of the Fire Control Radar (FCR)
2. Identify the basic components of the FCR
3. Discuss facts and principles of the FCR
   a. What happens when someone fails to follow the technical order (Integrity first)
   b. Tell about how we sometimes work longer hours in the repair phase (Service before self)
4. Discuss theory of operation of the FCR

There would be more to it, but I think you can see the point. The goal here is to pass on the technical information to the student while at the same time, telling them how they should conduct themselves once they graduate from the course. It is a way of setting a bedrock of behavior for the student that will help them as they progress through their career in working on the FCR. They not only learn how the system operates, but they also learn how to perform as leaders in their career field going forward, through real examples given to them by the instructor.

While conducting this eight-hour lecture, after identifying and discussing the operating principles of the FCR, I might have continued the lesson with something like this:

> When you're out on the line performing an operational checkout on the radar, remember that you will need to cordon off the area while transmitting. This is for the safety of all personnel in the area and is mandated in the technical orders. By following the technical orders, you are showing that you practice integrity first, which is expected of all maintainers. After all, one of our goals in maintenance is to provide safe, reliable aircraft for our pilots, and having the integrity to follow the technical orders ensures this happens.

I know this sounds kind of cheesy, but it works, and it also made for good filler over eight hours. One can only talk about pulse repetition frequencies and Doppler shifts for so long. But I digress. The important point here is to understand that as teachers and coaches, we must go above and beyond our lesson plans and lectures to find ways to help our students better understand and retain the content. Additionally, we want to display to them the leadership they deserve, even if they do not think they need it.

Students may not think they need leadership, and may not be looking for it in the classroom. But as the instruction goes on, a leader/follower relationship builds between the teacher and student. Therefore, teachers and coaches must maintain and display the characteristics of a leader. It becomes a bonus for the student, to learn about leadership. This is the reason students sometimes seek out their teachers, often years after graduation, to thank them for what they did for them. They remember because of the impact the teacher made on their lives. They recognized the leadership, even though they may have not been looking for it at the time. If this is the case, then it is likely they have adapted their teacher's leadership characteristics and have become a leader in their own right.

Back to the reluctant learner. I have a great example of an entire group of reluctant learners. One of the most challenging tasks I faced as an instructor in the Air Force was to conduct cross-training of more than sixty personnel from one aircraft to another. It was up to me and one other instructor to convert these sixty people from the MQ-1 Predator unmanned aerial vehicle into the F-16 Fighting Falcon. And it was quite a task, for sure.

The maintainers were being forced to cross-train into my career field, and not everyone was happy about it. The Air Force had decided to combine the Predator with the Falcon career fields, as far as avionics maintainers went. So, all these folks needed to go through my three-month class to learn about F-16 avionics. For three months, eight hours per day, I had four reluctant students in my classroom. Our instruction was very close-knit if you will, and as such required no more than four students per instructor ratio. This meant that the other instructor and I taught this class, back-to-back, for more than two years.

The reason for the students being so reluctant was because of their Air Force background. The Predator was relatively new at the time, and to field those maintenance vacancies, the Air Force forcibly cross-trained avionics technicians from large planes. Those folks worked on KC-135 and C-5 aircraft, for example, and were considered in a 'conventional' avionics career field. This meant that they typically worked from a back-shop, and did not need to interact with other maintainers on the flight line. They would be dispatched from their shop out to repair an aircraft, and then return when done. It was very different with the Predator, however.

The Predator was a very small, unmanned aerial vehicle, worlds different from a KC-135 or C-5. While some of the avionics systems were similar at least in theory, the method for performing maintenance on them was very different from what these maintainers were accustomed to. Some had been in their original career field for more than a decade and now had to cross-train. Maintenance on the Predator required every career field to be on the flight line, working together while launching, recovering, and performing maintenance on that aircraft. So, it was a difficult transition for many if not most of them. And then the Air Force pivoted a couple of years later and added them to the F-16 avionics career field. For some, this made it worse for them, in their minds.

The reason that it was worse for them was that while they had to work on the Predator, at least it was stationed at only one Air Force base. Sure, they had to deploy at times, but everyone in the Air Force does that. With the F-16, there was the uncertainty of where they could become stationed, as this aircraft was placed at bases all over the world. The one place most didn't like being stationed in was South Korea. This is what made them ultra-reluctant to become F-16 maintainers.

The F-16 maintenance community is relatively small. Most people who work on the F-16 will find themselves stationed at one of two Air Force bases in Korea. These assignments are referred to as 'remote' tours because they are completed without any family. The Air Force member must move there for one year without their family. With the community being so small, it is not unheard of that people get assigned there, multiple times in a career. I was stationed there twice. I've also known some people who have been stationed in Korea five separate times.

This is what made the cross-trainees so reluctant. They did not want any part of Korea, nor did they want any part in the maintenance concepts that were required to work on the F-16. Working avionics on the F-16 was not a back-shop environment at all. Everyone was on the flight line. As with the Predator, all worked together to launch, recover, and repair aircraft daily. This was not what they wanted, and they continuously let me know this. Talk about a challenge for me and the other instructor!

More than two years with reluctant, disinterested students, and it was tough at times. I remember during one of my lectures, one of the students was not paying attention. He blatantly stated during class that he wanted nothing to do with this aircraft, and was not interested in learning about it. So, I told him:

> You need to listen to what I am trying to teach you because you may be going to Korea once you're done here. And guess what? I'm not going to be an instructor forever, and will probably get stationed in Korea again. So, there is a chance that you and I become stationed there together, which means you could be working for me. If that happens, I'll know that you can work on an F-16, because I'm the one who taught you.

A little taken aback by my statement, he reluctantly began paying more attention, and successfully completed the course.

About a year later, I walked into the Specialist Flight office in the 36th Fighter Squadron at Osan Air Base, Korea as the new flight chief. Sitting there in the office with the other avionics guys was my reluctant student. His face fell when he saw me, and I asked him if he remembered what I had told him in class that day. He nodded. It turned out that he was a good technician and junior Non-Commissioned Officer, it was just that he needed some leadership to not only learn what I had to teach him but also put it into practice. He did so right in front of me, as he worked with me for several months at Osan before moving on to his next assignment.

Reluctant learners are tough, believe me. But if we keep up with the constant display of our leadership traits and characteristics, we can be assured that they will come around, eventually. I've seen it happen. This is especially important in this age of COVID.

The age of COVID requires many teachers to conduct their classes over the Internet via video conference calls. This can be extremely difficult and contributes to students becoming reluctant learners. Just think about what our teachers have endured through this time. They are expected to keep the student's attention span while having zero control over their personal areas. Teachers have always been accustomed to having the command of a classroom, where he or they can exert control over their students' attentiveness.

Not having the appropriate control of the classroom must be quite a difficult challenge for our teachers everywhere! I use the word 'control,' but it shouldn't be misconstrued as a bad thing. Part of being a successful teacher is controlling the room. The teacher must have the attention of the students, so they can get their lessons delivered and hopefully, understood. It is extremely difficult to do this when the teacher has no control.

So, if the students become disengaged, the teacher has lost control of the room. This could be the age of COVID's one-word definition of a reluctant learner: Disengaged. It is up to the teachers to influence the students to want to learn (like leadership, right?). Doing so from a video conference is extremely difficult. But we also must understand that being disengaged isn't the only thing that compels someone to become a reluctant learner. Aside from COVID, we still must deal with other commonly known reasons why someone is disinterested in the content. A student might simply be stubborn, or are interested in the subject, but are not understanding it due to other internal forces. The next chapter will expand on this by explaining a task that every teacher and coach is very familiar with: *One-On-One Time.*

One-On-One Time

A teacher affects eternity; he can never tell where his influence stops. — Henry Adams

In the last chapter, we discussed reluctant learners, and how difficult it can be to bring them into the fold and teach them what they need to learn. Sometimes, reluctant learners are this way not because they might be stubborn, rather because they simply don't understand the material. If this occurs, the student may end up retreating into a shell. This is where the teacher earns his or her money. They earn it by recognizing when a student needs specialized assistance to understand the content. It can be a special experience for a teacher, where it becomes very satisfying when they spend extra time, one-on-one with a student.

When the student finally understands, the teacher can see it. The teacher figuratively watches the light bulb over the student's head begin to illuminate. Once the student understands, and the teacher knows that they were able to help, everything gets better. The relationship between teacher and student improves as the student begins to show newfound respect for the teacher.

Taking on a student one-on-one is extremely important in teaching, and it is something that most if not all teachers will do. A recent survey showed that sixty-five percent of respondents spent between three and six hours of extra time with students requiring one-on-one attention. Some spent more time, but every respondent said they spent at least three hours of extra time with students. This is critical to the learning process. When a teacher sits with a student one-on-one, they also learn about the student. They might learn why he or she does not understand the content.

My example of this comes from my time as an instructor in the U.S. Air Force. Teaching from technical documents, we always looked through the books to reference whatever subject I was lecturing on. I gave reading assignments and had the students look up information to provide answers either orally or written.

During one class, I noticed an Airman who seemed to be having trouble finding the chapter that I asked him to reference. He was confused by my request. So, I mentioned to him to look it up in the Table of Contents, where he could easily find the page number to go to. He was also confused by this statement and asked what a Table of Contents was. He had never heard that term before!

I immediately sent the class on break and asked the Airman to remain behind. I sat with him and discussed the Table of Contents. After our short discussion, he was then familiar with what it was and what it meant. He did not have much of an academic background before joining the Air Force. But I was there to show him, as was my job as his instructor. But also, it was my job as a leader, to show him the way. I did not belittle him for not knowing something as common as a Table of Contents, rather, I explained to him what it was, and showed him how to use it. I also did this in a private, one-on-one session while the rest of the class was on break. I certainly didn't want to embarrass the young man, so it was the right thing to do and sit with him one-on-one.

I could tell that he was relieved by our discussion. When the class resumed, he was fine and easily adapted to my requests. He was able to keep up with the reading, contributed to the class, and graduated with his classmates.

This was only a quick example, but teachers and coaches do this daily to ensure their students and players comprehend the material. Doing so will ultimately ensure the students and players become successful in their learning experience. Teachers and coaches do this because they care. They care about their students and players because they want them to succeed. It is the same way in business.

In business, we want our subordinates, coworkers, and followers to be successful in their careers. We as leaders in the middle, can take a page from teachers and coaches everywhere, and ensure this occurs through our one-on-one conversations. Sometimes a follower needs correcting, sometimes he or she simply needs to learn more about their job. It is up to each of us to ensure we are doing everything we can for them. If we need to take additional time out of our day to sit with someone, then so be it. We do this because we want our followers to succeed in their own careers. We also do this because when a follower knows he or she is being cared about by their leader, they will ultimately become happier employees. This will also affect the company's bottom line, which leads to its success.

The teacher, coach, or leader must recognize when their students, players, or followers are having a difficult time. Whether it is academic content or a difficult task at hand, they may be bothered by something more personal. It might be something different from having trouble learning or completing said task. They might just be having a bad day, or it could be worse. It is up to us to recognize this and to handle it appropriately.

This falls into the realm of getting to know our people. Additionally, they need to get to know us. It is healthy for leader/follower relationships to become familiar, personally, with one another. It helps to build the trust required to work together toward a shared goal. Sometimes, just a funny or embarrassing story about what happened to us in a previous life will break the ice and develop positive, healthy relationships between the two. Doing so tends to bring one another to a common viewpoint. If we find that we have something in common with our followers, we become more apt to relate to them and their plight. And now, my embarrassing story.

Have you ever hit yourself between the eyes as hard as you could with a speed handle?

If you think this reads like an opening line to an embarrassing story, then you are correct. But I have a great reason for sharing. You see, once I had a coworker who was having a very bad day, and I felt the need to step in and try to cheer him up. I needed to be there for him and make him feel different about his day. We all have our bad days, but if we (as leaders) can make a difference to somebody, then we should take every opportunity to do so. This is what leadership looks like in action. If it took me telling an embarrassing story about myself, then so be it.

It had to be done because when I saw what he was going through, I became concerned about him as any leader would. I wanted to divert his attention away from what was digging at him and give him something to laugh about, something to ease his mind as he went about his day. I felt that I needed to be there for him. He had a job to do and was doing it well, although with a touch of aggression and forced will, to complete the task at hand.

I went into his office and closed the door so we could be alone. I asked him if it were okay for me to come in and sit with him while he worked. He was doing physical work which made it easy to have a conversation while remaining on task. I told him I was 'hiding' from my responsibilities and that I wanted to come in here with him to shoot the bull if he didn't mind.

Truth be told, I was being pulled in six different directions that morning, but I recognized that he needed some attention even though he may not have realized it at the time. I decided to delay my responsibilities so I could attend to his needs. In reality, I simply wanted to sit with him and allow him to unload some of his troubles upon me if he desired to do so. To 'vent,' if you will. He said he was happy for me to join him.

He talked as he worked, telling me about his morning, including all the stuff that had irritated him right from the start. I sat and listened, and offered casual conversation. I sensed that he needed a pick-me-up, a change in attitude, so I decided to tell him my story by stating, "Have you ever hit yourself between the eyes as hard as you could with a speed handle?"

A little surprised, he shook his head, smiling. "No." So I told him my story.

I was an aircraft maintainer in the U.S. Air Force for twenty-five years. Some of my work involved performing maintenance on the avionics systems of the F-16 Fighting Falcon fighter jet. One day as a young Airman, I was tasked to go out to a hangar and remove a lower UHF/IFF antenna from an aircraft. This antenna is about eight inches tall and looks like a shark fin. Attached to the aircraft by eight 'high-torque' screws, it is aerodynamically sound thanks to the thick sealant applied on the head of each screw along with aircraft paint.

Situated near the back of the aircraft, between the ventral fins, it is usually a simple job for any technician. By sitting cross-legged on the hangar floor, I could easily access the antenna right in front of my face as it pointed down from the fuselage. Its location on the aircraft makes it the cause of many a *Falcon Bite*, which occurs when a maintainer or pilot contacts it using his or her head. Doing this always leaves a mark, for sure. But I didn't get a Falcon Bite, as I had carefully navigated my way into position near the antenna. However, I was about to receive a wrench bite of epic proportions!

I got down to business by first using a metal pick to dig out as much of the aircraft paint and sealant that I could to free up the screw heads for my tool of choice, the speed handle. A speed handle is a wrench used to quickly remove screws. It is very familiar to aircraft maintainers, as they remove and install screws by the hundreds on an ongoing basis. The tool is a heavy piece of steel, cylindrical with a spinning handle on one end and a 3/8-inch drive on the other. A bit holder fits onto this end, and in that, fits a 'torque tip' bit used to remove and install screws.

Having dug out all the sealant, I next moved into position to begin removing the eight screws. These were high-torque screws that had been set into the mounting surface extremely tight. Not even one was planning to come out easily. Of course! Why would it be easy? The screws had obviously been over-torqued when they were initially installed. I realized that I needed to get more leverage onto the screw head, so I repositioned myself right next to the antenna and crouched up onto one knee. I bent my wrist back and laced my hand through the speed handle so that I could push up into the first screw head while twisting the handle counterclockwise with my wrist. Still, it would not budge.

Now, putting even more pressure up onto the screw head, the tip of the business end of the speed handle was a mere three inches away from my face. I was staring at the torque tip as I pushed, now sweating a little with the physical exertion. Pushing and twisting…pushing, twisting…pushing, twist…CLICK…WHACK! The torque tip shattered to pieces, and the tremendous force that I had been applying through the speed handle onto the torque tip was immediately transferred, directly to my face. WHACK! Right between the eyes. I saw stars and could have sworn that I heard a harmonic chiming, resonating from the speed handle as it vibrated the remainder of its torquing energy into space.

I sat back onto my butt and rolled out from under the aircraft. I yowled an expletive at the top of my lungs and threw the speed handle across the hangar, clattering it across the floor and scattering the bit holder and torque tip remnants in every direction. After a couple of minutes of calming breaths with my head in my hands, I finally got up and walked over to the bathroom adjacent to the hangar space. I looked in the mirror and saw myself looking back wearing a giant welt across the right side of my nose, up through the bridge between my eyes, and onto my forehead. It looked like a badge of honor…or stupidity, I don't know which. But oh boy did that smart!

I spent the next several minutes searching for the tiny parts that used to be a torque tip. You see, in aircraft maintenance, every tool must be accounted for, even broken ones. This is due to aircraft safety of flight. We need to know where our tools are located, broken or not. Once I finally found everything, I called for help to remove the screws. The sheet metal shop technicians eventually arrived and ended up drilling out the offending screw. Some of them were able to be removed by using a 'Johnson' bar, which is a tool for removing screws using an incredible amount of leverage, and a hammer wrench. An hour or so later, I was finally able to replace the antenna and install the eight high-torque screws, ensuring they were torqued to the printed specifications!

My coworker had a smile on his face the entire time I told my story. I had offered him a few minutes to disconnect from his rough morning and enjoy a laugh with me (at my expense). Yes, my story was a little embarrassing, but that is okay. As leaders, we must be ready to poke a little fun at ourselves from time to time. As I said, we all have our bad days. If a leader can make a positive difference in someone's day, then he or she has gone a long way toward earning their trust as well as their followership.

Taking the time to sit with a follower one-on-one is a noble and necessary matter for every person in a leadership role. As leaders in the middle, we must be able to connect with our followers on a personal basis. Doing so will help to create the bonds required to travel together toward our shared goal. This is especially important in teaching or coaching, where we will sometimes encounter students or players who do not understand the material or are falling behind for some other personal reason. It is up to the teacher or coach to recognize when this happens, and to then, take the time to sit one-on-one with them. It is here, where they will deliver specialized individual training, or simply relate an embarrassing story to make their day better.

When we talk with a student or follower one-on-one, we show them that we care for them. Showing that we care for someone is a sign of a competent leader, and is one of the traits that I outline in the next chapter, *Five Traits of a Leader in the Middle.*

Five Traits of a Leader in the Middle

Leadership and learning are indispensable to each other. — John F. Kennedy

A s the previous chapter explained, sitting one-on-one with a follower and having a conversation with them is a necessary part of being a leader. Teachers and coaches do this constantly as a part of their job. But to do so and mean it, shows that it really isn't just part of a job, rather it shows that a teacher or coach is practicing the leadership traits of care and communication. People are more apt to follow someone who exhibits certain leadership traits, and these two traits are valuable in helping leaders find success in cultivating followers.

Communication is probably the number one leadership trait that anyone must have in their leadership toolbox. But this is arguable for sure because numerous leadership traits exist. It is up to the leader to figure out which ones to acquire and how to best utilize them. A quick Internet search will reveal numerous sources that identify many leadership traits. Depending on what is found, a dozen or more traits are explained. The traits I believe I identify with the most are listed below:

Communication (includes active listening, responding, and articulating)
Energy (being present)
Care
Empathy
Trustworthiness

As you go through each of these traits, think about how they apply to your situation, whether your profession is as a teacher, coach, or shift lead in a manufacturing department. The point is, no matter where you are on the corporate ladder, if you want to be a leader, you must be able to influence those around you to go in your direction; specifically, to *want* to go in your direction. So, read how these traits work for me, and then do some independent research to learn more about these and other traits. You should then be able to determine which ones work best for you.

Communication

As said before, communication is probably the number one trait to possess. I say this because as a leader, we must be able to talk to our potential followers. Since communication itself is a wide-ranging subject, in this instance I will focus on verbal communication. This includes active listening, properly responding, and finally, articulating the proper message to the followers.

Active listening is critical to showing a potential follower that we are truly paying attention to what is being said. This is critical because if we do not listen to what they say, they will decide not to follow. Active listening means that the listener must stay on point and give his or her full attention to what the follower is saying, much like the example of Chuckie providing instruction to the F-16 student pilot. This can be done by:

Being ready to listen
Providing positive nonverbal responses
Providing meaningful feedback

Being ready to listen means that the leaders should make all efforts to make the speaker feel welcomed. Should he or she feel welcome, they will be more apt to open up and trust the leader with their thoughts. This is done by taking some very simple steps. The conversation should take place in a private room, if possible. There should be no 'barriers to communication' like distractions on a desk. These distractions are anything from computer monitors to office supplies, picture frames, coffee cups, etcetera, placed on the desk between the two participants. Sometimes, just sitting in front of their leader's desk will intimidate the follower. A way to fix this is to simply move away from the desk or to a different location altogether.

I once had an opportunity to go and speak with a senior director in my company. When I went into his office to meet him, he immediately got out from behind his desk, stepped around it, and greeted me warmly. Next, he invited me to sit with him at the two chairs he had previously positioned, away from his desk. His not staying behind his desk is my point. By moving to a different location (even within his office) he made me feel comfortable about the conversation we were about to have. He had ensured that I would feel comfortable in my visit with him by removing any barriers to communication.

Once we have become ready to listen, we must actually listen—what a concept! We can show the speaker that we are listening by providing nonverbal feedback to them as they speak. This is also very easy. Providing nonverbal feedback is as simple as keeping eye contact and smiling as they talk. Well, not always smiling, right? They might be telling us about a serious occurrence in their life that does not warrant a smile in response. If we sit there smiling while they tell of the car accident from the night before, they will immediately know that we do not care about their message. We are not listening! So, we must use facial expressions wisely, such as providing a smile when warranted, as well as a look of concern or even frowning, based upon what we are hearing.

Another form of nonverbal feedback is how we position our bodies; our body language, per se. While sitting in the conversation, we should refrain from crossing our arms or even leaning back in our chair. Leaning forward in the chairs shows that we are interested in what is being said. Entire courses have been taught on this aspect of communication, alone.

The final part of active listening is providing meaningful feedback. This is probably the most difficult aspect of the communication process. What do we say when a follower presents us with a serious personal problem? Knowing that each situation is different, as leaders we must be able to give the appropriate responses which will help the follower in their unique situation. At times, the leader may not be qualified to respond, such as those required by a qualified therapist or counselor. In these instances, the best thing to do is to refer the person to a professional and then, support them the entire way. But in an everyday conversation where the follower is asking for answers that the leader is qualified to answer, they must be able to properly articulate the answer to them.

This takes practice! To properly respond to the follower, the leader must have experience in the subject matter. If the leader has no clue what he is talking about and yet tries to respond, the follower will detect it immediately and begin to lose respect for the leader. So, the leader must have the knowledge required to make a response. And then, the leader must be able to relay it in such a way that it makes sense to the follower. Talk in plain English (or whatever language), so as not to talk over their head or 'down' to them. Do not ramble, rather stay on point. Talk friendly, talk openly, and most of all, talk honestly. Being open and honest are also very good traits to being an effective leader.

While more concepts and levels exist in the art of communication, using these three points I have explained here will be very helpful to anyone interested in becoming a better leader. Being ready to listen, providing the correct nonverbals, and then articulating proper responses to the follower, are paramount to the success of communication as a leader in the middle.

<u>Energy</u>

To have energy as a leader means we must be present. What I mean by this is that every day we must be present in our mind, body, and spirit while at our workplace. Everyone has their bad days, but for us to be successful as a leader, we must have the ability to look past the bad days and handle the task at hand. It can be very difficult to pay attention to a follower in need if we are distracted by our foul moods or personal faults. The reason for this is because as the leader, we are there for them. We are there to provide for our followers when they need us. We will have a difficult time doing so if we are not present.

Having energy is important, but we must ensure we don't overdo it. I had a supervisor in the U.S. Air Force a long time ago who was a great leader but sometimes took his energy levels too far. Our squadron had been preparing to begin a wartime exercise scenario, which involved the entire Air Force base for a week. Nobody ever looked forward to these types of exercises because they were extremely strenuous and involved long hours, often wearing a chemical warfare ensemble which was very uncomfortable. These exercises always began with a telephone 'recall,' which was when every person in the squadron received a call from their supervisor telling them to report to work immediately.

I was awakened by my phone ringing off its hook at four in the morning. After I sleepily answered the phone, the voice at the other end was my supervisor telling me in a most upbeat and enthusiastic way,

"Good morning Sergeant Boling! Welcome to our recall, I'll see you at work soon!" I could almost picture his exuberant face, smiling broadly as he called me into work. He was always like that, laughing and smiling with every unpopular task he delegated. Don't get me wrong; he was a good supervisor and leader, but it seemed to me that he kind of overdid it sometimes. His energetic manner did not work for everyone. Some people never respond to his spirited leadership style and were somewhat annoyed by it. So as leaders, we must be able to find a balance and not overdo it. Having energy is very important, but we must temper it so we don't drive them away.

Another way to be present and display the energy required is to get out from behind our desks and walk around the facility. When followers see the leader getting around and being with them, they tend to feel better about following him or her. This is also referred to as Leadership by Walking Around or LBWA. Leaders should practice this whenever they get the chance because doing so will not only make the follower feel better about a given situation, it is also healthy for the leader to do it!

By having the energy to be present in their followers' work lives, the leader is displaying to them that he or she cares. This leads me to the next trait, care.

Care

I think this trait might be on par with communication, as far as importance goes. When we care about something or somebody, it shows. If we make an effort to care about our followers, our workplace, and our mission, the people will respond appropriately. If the followers know and understand that their leader cares about them, they will respond in many ways. Mostly, they will respond by performing better in their jobs. They respond by wearing smiles on their faces, enjoying their work environment, and finally, they respond by positively working toward the organization's goals. In short, they care, too.

Caring for our followers is extremely important as a leader in the middle. When we care about them, it shows. This is because as the leader, we are always on display. Our followers are always watching us, and if they detect that the leader does not seem to care about the people, they will surely cease to follow. This is because leadership practice, both good and bad, is always on display for all to see. The people know, and they will make the appropriate choice. So, it is imperative that as leaders, we care about our people, workplace, and mission. It matters.

Empathy

An extremely important trait to have is empathy toward our follower's plight. 'Walking in one's shoes' is critical to understanding when a follower is going through a rough patch in their life. This trait kind of melds together with communication and caring, because to express empathy is to show the follower that we care about their situation while we converse with them.

When a follower comes to us with a problem, we must show that we care about them and their problem by empathizing with them. Doing so will also help the leader to understand what is occurring, and allow them to make a comparison to any possible similar circumstances the leader had in his or her past life. When we make an understanding such as this, we are more able to respond appropriately to the follower.

People need empathetic leaders in their lives. When someone comes to us with their troubles, it shows that they trust us to help them in their time of need. When someone does this, it is incredibly humbling to be the person they chose to confide in. By displaying empathy toward their plight, we are giving them an idea of hope. This will go a long way toward resolving their trouble. Leaders with empathy help to make this happen.

Trustworthiness

Being trustworthy displays to the followers that we as the leader may hold their troubles in confidence. Trustworthy leaders won't gossip or handle critical situations as trivial. Additionally, trustworthy leaders will be there for their followers and will do everything in their power to make it right for their followers.

Being trustworthy means that the leader is ethical, honest, and dependable. These words are leadership traits in their own respect. So, by being a trustworthy leader, not only are we expressing this trait, but also the traits of ethics, honesty, and dependability. When you think about it, to be trustworthy is to wrap up all these traits into one neat package. This includes some of the traits I have listed before, including care and empathy.

For a follower to trust the leader is huge! If the follower cannot trust their leader, how can we expect them to bring their troubles to us? How can we empathize with them if they will not come to us in the first place? If they will not come to us, how can we show them that we care? If we don't talk to them or show a somewhat energetic attitude with them, they'll not follow at all.

~ ~ ~

You should see that there is a pattern in this. All five of the traits I have listed here are connected in some respect, as each trait compliments one another. For instance, we cannot display empathy if we don't ever take the chance to communicate with them. We cannot tell them we care if we are not present to display even the slightest bit of energy. And of course, if we say or do things that make them not trust us, how can we be a leader at all?

We should apply these traits in our professions the same way that teachers and coaches do in theirs. Many if not all these traits are included in the mental makeup of teachers and coaches everywhere. We should think about how we relate to these traits and identify any other traits that we espouse. Think about them, and see how we can adapt these traits and others, into our professions. This is how we become more successful as leaders in the middle.

When I determined the traits for this chapter, I sat and pondered how I felt about my leadership style. The words that came to me, communication, energy, care, empathy, and trustworthiness, were the ones that stood out in my mind of how I felt I behaved at work with respect to my coworkers, supervisors, and followers. As I go through each day with my team, I try to stay true to these five traits. Sure, sometimes it can be difficult, depending on the circumstances. But if I want to continue to be considered as a leader in my area (the middle), then I need to live these traits every day.

It can be difficult to stay the course because our emotions can sometimes get the best of us and we do have our bad weeks. But I try. I had to utilize some of these traits recently, where I had the opportunity to address a bit of trouble at work. A situation had occurred where my team had questions about some recent management decisions in the workplace, as well as questions about my role in them, specifically. Unknowingly, I had walked into the room where an impromptu team meeting was taking place. They polled me about their concerns, and I listened to them. They tried to get a feel about my contributions to the team and were concerned about some recent issues that involved me.

I explained what had been going on in my week, being very transparent and honest. I described that I had a discussion with the manager about it and that I had made my points to him of my concerns. To address their concern about my contributions, I said that my work involved a lot of 'behind the scenes' stuff, that they may not see every day. This was information that they already knew, but a clearly stated reiteration was in order. I then said to them, "*Everything I do here, I do for you.*" I wanted to make it very clear to them that I cared for each one of them.

Their nonverbal feedback told me everything I needed to know. They were with me. They all stayed positive and accepted my words. They had been a little concerned about recent happenings in the workplace, and I was able to relieve them of their concerns. This little ten-minute impromptu meeting helped me and my team to go further in our leader-follower relationship. So, thinking about these leadership traits and successfully utilizing them in this situation was a great feeling, which turned negative feelings into positive ones. But these particular traits may not work for everyone, so luckily there are many more to choose from.

Of course, this list of five traits is not all-inclusive. Numerous leadership traits exist, and it is up to the individual to choose which ones they feel they can use the easiest. I believe it falls to the person's personality, as to which leadership trait becomes more familiar. But it is highly imperative to develop the traits that we are comfortable with so that we can be there for our followers. This is important because if we choose not to develop leadership traits, we will never become a leader at all.

These five traits are very important in the ongoing development of a leader in the middle. Every teacher and coach possesses them, or some similar form, to be successful in their profession. One of these traits, care, seems to keep coming up in my leadership discussions and writing. The next chapter expands on it, even more, using a new acronym, GAS. Now, the *GAS Factor.*

The GAS Factor

Students don't care how much you know until they know how much you care. — Anonymous

How's your GAS factor nowadays? Oh no, not another acronym! In the military, it seemed we had an acronym for everything. In fact, my buddies and I used to carry on entire conversations using mostly acronyms. We would purposely do this during social gatherings outside of work, and would clearly understand each other. Most people around us, however, could not understand what we were saying. It was sort of like a secret code, one that only we flight line guys could understand. The main reason we did this was simply to irritate our wives.

At any rate, I've just come up with a new acronym that everyone should get to know, especially those who strive to be a leader. GAS stands for Give A Shit. Sorry (not sorry), but we sometimes used profanity in the military. So, how's your GAS factor nowadays? Is your tank full, empty, or somewhere in between?

This is one of those chapters that was written for more of a business environment, but the message should also be clearly understood regarding teachers and coaches. Every teacher or coach must have a full GAS tank or they will struggle in their profession. This pertains to what teachers and coaches do every day—they care about those they are charged with teaching or coaching. If a teacher or coach didn't care about their students or players, nothing would ever get accomplished. If the teachers and coaches didn't motivate their students and players into learning, nobody would be interested in learning anything.

What teachers and coaches experience and how they behave in their everyday work has a lot to do with non-teaching professions as well. My hope is for the reader to relate the experiences of these outstanding leaders to their own experiences and their own professions. Basically, how can we adapt what teachers and coaches do to our own situation? How do they compare?

A person's GAS factor is supremely important to the success of any organization. Whether the person is in management, an individual contributor, teacher, or coach, it matters. We should remember that wherever our mental attitude falls along the GAS gauge (full to empty), we should know that others around us are affected by our GAS factor. The fuller our gauge, the healthier our organization becomes. Each person's attitude toward their surroundings at work affects all colleagues around them. In some cases, as the gauge nears empty, a sour mood appears which can permeate the entire office. What if this sour mood is generated by the manager or teacher himself?

As the manager's GAS gauge nears empty, the whole office suffers. As the leader of the office, it is up to him or her to set the example for others to follow. But in some cases, they just can't help it. Their positive attitude wanes as their GAS factor decreases. This can be caused by almost anything in the person's personal or professional life. Personally, he or she might be worried or distracted by events on the home front, such as financial standing or health issues. Professionally, they may become frustrated or disappointed by many aspects of the job, such as a perceived lack of power or control by those from above. Numerous reasons exist for these frustrations in any company, but if there seems to be no light at the end of the tunnel for the manager or teacher, then his or her attitude will begin to fall along with those around him.

A monkey wrench to throw in here is the fallout from the worldwide pandemic of COVID-19. This disaster has made everything difficult, to the point of wearing a mask or face shield any time we go out in public. Notwithstanding the horrible aspect of the possibility of our loved ones dying, we all have had to deal with this pandemic in our own ways. In a professional environment as well as in the classroom or on the playing field, it is up to the manager, teacher, or coach to lead their folks and do the right thing.

It is imperative in this time of COVID-19 that teachers and coaches have a full GAS tank, especially because of their daunting responsibility of leading and teaching their students and players during the pandemic. Nobody likes conducting (or attending) class over Zoom or working under a face shield or mask. Yet, it is up to each teacher and coach to lead their students and players through this uncomfortable and unprecedented time.

From my research, I have seen that many teachers and coaches are doing just that, which is the key reason for my writing this book in the first place. Teachers and coaches have accepted the awesome responsibility of leading their students and players through this pandemic, and most are performing admirably. What they do for us as a society, every day is downright noble. Parents and school administrators have placed their trust in them, and as such are counting on them to be the 'leaders in the middle' that we all know them to be. Students and players look to them for the guidance they need to be successful. The same goes in non-teaching organizations; the employees need their managers to lead them through this trying time.

If the teacher, coach, or manager's tank is empty, the tanks of his or her students, players or employees empty out, too. This is because followers look to their leader to show them the way. If a leader outwardly displays his disdain for the company or the current work situation, then the followers will begin to feel it as well. As students, players, or individual contributors, these followers have their own types of frustrations and disappointments to deal with. Personal distractions aside, professionally, a myriad of reasons exist for them to feel their tanks draining.

Maybe they didn't get that promotion they were counting on, or they were having trouble completing tasks without the proper tools to do their job. Maybe they were under quarantine or were worried about their loved ones' health. The after-effects of COVID-19 have hit everybody negatively. These and numerous other distractions and reasons can be identified, which may bring a student, player, or employee down. But when the leader does it too, it makes it that much more difficult to recover.

For instance, I faced a personal quandary last year, due to COVID. I ended up canceling Father's Day 2020. My kids and grandson were planning on a big day with us celebrating, but I canceled it. What put the double whammy on this decision was that day was also our thirty-fourth wedding anniversary. So, not only were the kids disappointed but so was my wife. I made this tough decision to cancel because the virus had had a resurgence in my state in only one week. I felt it was the right thing to do, although it had gotten me down, to help keep my family safe.

The world had been dealing with this pandemic for half a year by then, and from my vantage point, it had been a somewhat distant threat for me and my family. Once the initial self-quarantining abated, we started getting back to our normal routines and lives. This was done little by little, but it was beginning to feel almost normal. Then this resurgence began happening in Arizona and it started hitting a lot closer to home for us, both personally and at work. I could sense the worry from my coworkers as the news of increased cases started to spread once again. So, I made my decision.

My decision wasn't made because of my coworkers, but their plight had influenced me. I gathered the facts, listened to my coworkers, spoke with my wife, and came to a personal decision. It wasn't made flippantly or off the cuff, but careful thought had gone into it. It brings me to this:

A sense of leadership is required to make tough decisions

As leaders, we are faced with making tough decisions daily. This is what we need in today's society: the leadership required to make tough decisions.

This is true any time but is most important right now with the pandemic, murders, protests, riots, and this ridiculous *cancel culture* that has materialized from it all. I am not suggesting that leadership must be displayed from those at the top, rather from those of us in the middle. Those at the top are already doing the right things from what I've seen. Military commanders, company CEOs, senior vice presidents, directors, and senior managers are doing their best to deal with this tough situation. They are making the strides required to get their respective areas of responsibility in order.

But what about those of us in the middle? What are we doing at our level? I've said before that leaders exist at every level of every organization, worldwide. Most leaders are right here in the middle, with me. So, what are we doing to deal with this tough situation? Something we leaders in the middle can do is to take charge of our areas of responsibility, both personally and professionally. We should ensure that those who count on us can get the answers they need, and have someone to look to in times of trouble.

One of the basic tenets of leadership in situations like this is caring for our people. As leaders, we need to care more. We need to maintain a full

GAS tank. We need to care for those we are charged with leading, whether it be at work or home. If we truly care about them, then we are more apt to step up and make those tough decisions. Leaders take charge, even at the middle level. To do this, I believe we should be open to learning more about leadership. In times of trouble, people look to their leaders, as mentioned. Why not become one of these leaders for our people, for our families?

Let's learn more about leadership, shall we? We need to search for leadership opportunities and education. Buy the books, follow the Twitter handles, learn as much as we can. If we do these things, we will learn about ourselves, too. We will learn that we have become able to gather up the courage to make difficult decisions, like canceling Father's Day or a thirty-fourth wedding celebration.

If we learn these leadership skills and accept the awesome responsibility of being the leader for our coworkers and our families, we just might make a difference. We just might make a difference in their lives, and in a larger sense, make a difference in our communities. We just might even contribute to the overall healing of our country. But leadership is required first, and it starts here with us, the leaders in the middle. And we must keep our GAS tanks full.

So, how can we keep our GAS tanks full? This could be a difficult question to answer. As I said, numerous reasons are found which can bring down both leaders and followers. But it is up to each of us, leader and follower, to try and keep it full for the sake of our mental health! We must Give A Shit or we will seemingly never be happy in our professional lives. Understand that unhappiness in our professional lives may very well lead to unhappiness in our private lives as well. So, how do we keep our tanks full?

~ ~ ~

Here are some ideas that I believe will help the leader. It is slanted more toward non-teaching professions, but much of this also applies to teachers and coaches:

Be present

Being present means that the leader must be there for their followers. He or she needs to get out of the office and get to know their people. Get to know them, and let them know that you are there for them. Be present, be available, be genuine.

Provide empowerment

By empowering the workforce to complete tasks on their own with little pressure from above lends itself to success. Employees will begin to feel good about their job/task, and the organizational mood could rise to a higher level.

Be professional

Being professional means that the leader will treat each individual with respect. It also means that the leader should eliminate negative statements about the company or his woes or problems in front of the followers.

Recognize

The leader must recognize that he or she can only take care of what is right in front of them, and try not to worry about what is beyond their control. Different levels of management exist in every company for a reason. The leader must recognize that he or she can only control the tasks at their level, but understand that what they do may have ripples across the company (positive or negative).

Smile!

Remember that as the leader, everyone is watching their every move like a hawk. The non-verbal cues can make or break the successful development of a leader, which leads to the successful development of the overall organization.

Here are some ideas that I believe will help the follower. As above, it is slanted toward non-teaching organizations, but much of this also applies to students and players:

Do your job

Wow, that sounds harsh! But as followers, if they do their jobs properly and consistently, the company will tend to have success, as well as the overall health of the organization. Other followers are watching, and if employees do their jobs well, then others may follow along and do the same. Bill Belichick has been known to say, "Do your job," numerous times during his time as the head coach of the New England Patriots. Take it from a winner, do your job!

Set the example

Employees are not just followers. There are leaders among them too! We can lead from wherever we find ourselves in an organization. We do not have to be at the top. This is accomplished when we lead by example.

Recognize

Just as the leader must do, followers must recognize that they can only do what is in their purview. Employees usually have a more limited span of control than a manager, so they must recognize that they cannot fix everything. They can only take care of what is in their own court. However, just as in the case of the leader, employees should recognize that what they do does affect the success (or failure) of an organization.

Smile!

Again, just as the leader must do, employees should understand that their body language (positive or negative) is contagious to their coworkers. If an employee walks around with a dark cloud over his head, everyone will notice it. Believe it or not, when an employee does this, his coworkers tend to follow suit. So, understanding that nonverbal language is powerful, try to be positive whenever possible. The health of the organization depends on it.

~ ~ ~

Our GAS factor weighs heavily in the success or failure of a given organization. It is up to each of us; managers and employees, leaders and followers, teachers and students, coaches and players, to do the right things at work in the classroom and on the field. It is also imperative to understand that when we walk around with an empty GAS tank, others will notice. It is in the best interest of ourselves, as well as our organizations, to strive to improve our wellbeing in the workplace. Doing so will only result in success. So, how's your GAS factor nowadays? Is your tank full, empty, or somewhere in between? Let's fill 'er up!

Those who have full GAS tanks are most likely good leaders and/or followers. But how do they get there? How does one become a good leader? Well, it depends on many different things like adapting certain leadership theories, styles, or behaviors. Which theory/style/behavior works best for you? The next chapter, *Leadership Theories*, identifies four of them.

Leadership Theories

The mediocre teacher tells. The good teacher explains. The superior teacher demonstrates. The great teacher inspires. — William A. Ward

Numerous theories exist within the leadership continuum. Each is important, and each works well, depending upon circumstances. When it comes to teachers and coaches, I believe four theories (including their underlying styles) should be discussed. Each is significant, and each can work within the teaching or coaching realms, depending upon circumstances. As with most leadership styles, the usage of a particular one is dependent on the situation. This is very similar to the situational leadership theory of telling, selling, participating, and delegating.

This chapter will discuss these theories and put them into categories like the situational leadership model. As you read them, I ask you to think about teachers or coaches from your past and try to fit these folks into the model and see where they land. Also, try to place yourself into one or more of the categories, as this may help you to determine your leadership style, as well as which theories make sense to you. I hope that by doing so, you may realize a distinct potential in yourself that could help you in your professional development or personal situation. After all, we are all still learning, right?

The four leadership theories that I feel are the most prevalent in the teacher and coaching realm are as follows:

Transformational Theory or Authoritative Style
Transactional Theory or Autocratic Style
Servant Theory or Affiliative Style

Laissez-Faire Theory or Delegative Style

First, an explanation between theory and style should be provided, as I believe they are relatively interchangeable in a discussion about leadership. A leadership theory would be the overall thought process regarding leading. An umbrella of leadership thought if you will. A style would be the actual method of acting out the theory and falling under the umbrella. For instance, someone who espouses the transformational theory might take on an authoritative style in their daily approach to leadership. It is important to understand that many different styles can make up a transformational-thinking person. In the context of this discussion, both theories and styles might be used interchangeably.

I picked four theories because they each have different components to successful leadership within the classroom or playing field. Again, depending upon the situation, each can be used successfully. If we cut to the chase, just by looking at these theories, we can surmise that low-performing teachers and coaches might use a delegative style, while high-performing teachers and coaches might embody more of an authoritative style. But we are not here to surmise, we need to look at some definitions first.

Transformational Leadership

A process where leaders and their followers raise one another to higher levels of morality and motivation. -- James McGregor Burns

Transformational leadership is characterized by the leader and follower working together toward a shared goal. According to Bernard M. Bass, this kind of leader:

Is a model of integrity and fairness.

Sets clear goals.

Has high expectations.

Encourages others.

Provides support and recognition.

Stirs the emotions of people.

Gets people to look beyond their self-interest.

Inspires people to reach for the improbable.

The transformational leader has his or her follower's best interests at heart. It is important to these leaders to ensure that their followers achieve their best. They are also motivated to break the status quo and always look for ways to improve themselves or their environment. I would consider this leadership theory the pinnacle of leadership because it considers the people to be just as important as the task at hand. Yes, tasks need to be accomplished, but by utilizing this approach, the leader ensures that the followers are engaged to the fullest in completing the task.

Transformational leaders are also very charismatic and inspirational. Their followers look to them as role models in times of trouble or difficult circumstances. People seek out leaders like this. They may need to find that beacon of light, and many times it is their teacher or coach that provides this for them. Teachers and coaches are definitely role models for many people.

Lastly, this type of leader provides intellectual stimulation while also considering the individual's needs. Teachers and coaches provide the vision necessary to accomplish this goal, whether it be through lecturing, or sitting with the student one-on-one to provide individualized training or correction. This theory exemplifies teachers and coaches who are highly productive and successful.

Transactional Leadership

> A leadership style based on the setting of clear goals and objectives for followers and the use of rewards and punishments to encourage compliance. -- Max Weber

Transactional, or managerial, leadership is characterized by the leader telling the follower exactly what to do and is governed by rules. According to Bernard M. Bass, these kinds of leaders:

Revel inefficiency.
Very left-brained.
Tend to be inflexible.
Opposed to change.
Focused on short-term goals.
Favor structured policies and procedures.
Thrive on following rules and doing things correctly.

Transactional leadership is just that—a transaction. The leader gives an assignment, and the follower completes the assignment. This is widely used in the military, where officers give orders and the lower ranking individual carries them out without question. From a business standpoint, this type of leadership is where the manager gives the assignment and the employee executes it. When the assignment is complete, the employee receives a reward via salary or recognition. If the assignment is not completed correctly, the employee receives a punishment. In an academic environment, the teacher gives the assignment and the student completes it. In return, the appropriate grade is given.

Transactional leadership is very rigid and does not consider the person who is performing the task. In other words, correct task completion is more important than the feelings of the person completing it. This type of leadership can also be very successful, however, especially in a coaching environment. Coaches try to extract every ounce of effort from their players, with the ultimate reward becoming that of winning the game or championship. This leadership theory exudes a very competitive nature, albeit within a rigid set of rules. Leaders who practice this type of leadership prefer the status quo.

Servant Leadership

> The servant-leader is servant first...It begins with the natural feeling that one wants to serve, to serve first. -- Robert K. Greenleaf

Servant leadership is a theory that concentrates all efforts on the follower. Greenleaf further explains that these types of leaders encompass:

Empathy, healing.
Commitment to the growth and development of people.
Foresight, stewardship.
Listening, persuasion.
Building community.
Conceptualization, self-awareness.

Servant leaders care about their followers. They spend more effort ensuring their followers are happy and healthy than they do worrying about the task at hand. They aren't forgetting the task, rather, they know that if they take care of their followers, the task will be completed automatically. This is because when the followers are of a healthy mind and spirit, they will be more apt to complete the task correctly. They know their leader cares for them and this knowledge enables them to be more diligent in completing the tasks.

In a teacher/student relationship, this type of leadership theory professes that teachers care for their students. If the student senses this, they will be more apt to complete the assignment or learn the subject matter. Students may not admit it or even realize they are behaving in this manner, but still display an interest or even an eagerness to learn the subject matter. Some will do this simply to please their teacher. They want to make the teacher happy because they realize that the teacher is doing everything in his or her power to help the student to be successful. It becomes kind of a two-way street.

Many studies in servant leadership theory explain a typical leadership/organizational pyramid where the leader is at the top and the employees are at the bottom. This theory flips the script, if you will, and places the leader at the bottom. From the bottom, he or she supports those who work for them—their followers. So, the leader is working to help the employees succeed. In a sense of the teacher/student relationship, it can be seen in the same manner. The teacher is doing everything he or she can to support their students, to provide for them, and give them the knowledge required to ensure they become successful.

This also suggests a very typical manager/employee relationship. The employee works for the manager, right? Well, this theory suggests something different. The employee does not work for the manager; he works for himself, his coworkers, and his family. These are the people who count on him, so he works for them. By that same token, if a manager says, "You work for me," he is just being a boss. He is not a leader. Because a leader, a true servant leader, says, "You don't work for me; I work for you."

<u>Laissez-Faire Leadership</u>

> A philosophy or practice characterized by a usually deliberate abstention from direction or interference, especially with individual freedom of choice and action. -- Merriam-Webster

Laissez-Faire leadership is a very relaxed, almost anti-leadership theory. I have it included here as a theory, but for the most part, it is simply a delegative leadership style. However, it can still be utilized successfully. According to Kendra Cherry, this type of leadership exhibits:

> A strict hands-off approach.
> Leaders provide all training and support.
> Accountability falls to the leader.
> Decisions are left to employees.
> Leaders are comfortable with mistakes.

These delegative characteristics do not sound much like what would be practiced in a classroom, right? Well, in some instances they unfortunately are. But in a true academic environment, this type of leadership is not warranted. In business, however, this can sometimes be successful, sometimes not. As in every leadership theory or approach, it has its pros and cons.

Allowing a hands-off approach can encourage personal growth, but in an academic setting, the results are not realized quickly enough. Sure, every student must take the responsibility to grow personally, but if the teacher uses this approach, how is he or she going to ever know if it was successful? Personal growth can take years to come to fruition, so this type of theory is of the long-haul variety and thus, not as effective for teachers or coaches.

Now that we have identified these four types of leadership theories, let's put them together. This will take on the look at the situational leadership model I was referring to at the beginning of the chapter. We can take all four of these theories and associate them with how a leader will utilize a style based on two things: people and tasks. Each theory will correlate to how low or how high we value the people as well as the task at hand. Look at the diagram on the next page:

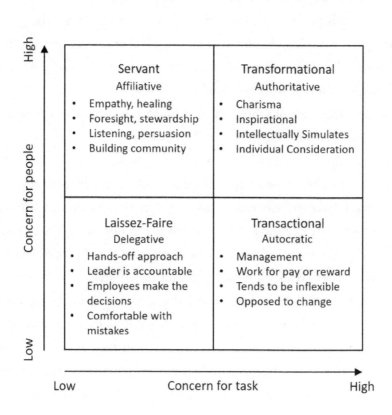

After studying the diagram, we can see that any of the theories or styles can be utilized successfully in the classroom or playing field, depending on the circumstances. For example, on the first day of school, let's say Sheldon Cooper from the CBS television show, *Young Sheldon* arrives in the classroom. Knowing he is a genius from the television show, the teacher can most certainly practice the Laissez-Faire theory and provide the young man with the textbook and assignments. The teacher knows that Sheldon will complete the delegated assignments on time and correctly without much if any, interaction from the teacher.

But what if the student who walked through the door was Jeff Spicoli from Universal Pictures' *Fast Times at Ridgemont High*? You may look it up or recall that Spicoli was the anti-student, a stoner surfer dude who couldn't care less about learning, or attending school for that matter. The teacher would have to carefully choose from one or more different theories (other than Laissez-Faire) to reach the young man. They would have to spend a great deal of attention on this student, and properly utilize transactional theory styles, along with servant theory styles.

Many examples can fit in here, and I think you can see the gist of it. What is important is how teachers and coaches can adapt their leadership styles to the situation in front of them. How can they most affect the student or player to help them reach their utmost potential in the learning process? It is through the proper usage of the leadership theories and styles presented here.

After reading this chapter, ask yourself how are you able to relate to it? Can you see yourself and your leadership style landing somewhere on the diagram? In my opinion, I would think that teachers would fall somewhere along the servant and transformational realms, while coaches would fall somewhere in the transactional and transformational realms. But it is important to understand that anyone can fall into any of these categories in their daily work, regardless of their profession. So, where do you fall? Once you determine this, are you making a difference in your students' or followers' lives?

We can utilize and practice all the leadership theories we want. But if we don't have the tools in which to do our jobs, what's the point in trying? Unfortunately, this is all too common in the teaching profession. Teachers and coaches are forced to dig into their own pockets to do their jobs. I have an opinion on this, which I explain in the next chapter, *The Deep Dive*.

The Deep Dive

Teachers are expected to reach unattainable goals with inadequate tools. The miracle is that at times they accomplish this impossible task. — Haim Ginott

How often have we dove deep into our own pockets to purchase items that were required for our work? Unfortunately, we sometimes must do this to get the job done, but it does happen. For some, it happens too often. Take school teachers, for instance. It has been well documented that many teachers go out-of-pocket to purchase classroom items like pencils and paper to support their curriculum. Parents and school districts help, but it always seems to fall onto the teacher to make it right for their students and to give them the best opportunity for success. Successful students tend to make the teacher happy, by bringing a sense of accomplishment to their efforts.

One of the thoughts of leadership that I have written about is how to make happy employees. A method for realizing this is to "Give 'em what they want; give 'em what they need." This means the manager should give his or her employees the tools they need to succeed; the tools they need to be happy in the workplace. Give them what they want, which is salary or recognition. Give them what they need, which is a safe working environment and the tools they need to do their jobs. For teachers, this includes pencils and paper. Unfortunately, budgetary restraints sometimes do not allow for it. So, are teachers unhappy in their work due to this constraint? Maybe. But I reckon that many if not most, are happy in their work, even if they must spend their own money to get the tools they need. This is because they care.

Teachers care so much for their students that they are willing to spend a portion of their salary to make their student's learning experiences better. A recent teacher and coach survey revealed that more than half of respondents typically spent between one hundred and five hundred dollars per year on school supplies. Twenty-two percent said they spent at least five hundred dollars per year. More than five hundred dollars per year is an astonishing number, but they do it because they care. They want to provide the best possible learning experience because their students deserve it. They do this because they are the leaders in their arena, the classroom. Now, let's look at this from a different perspective.

Take any common workplace, for instance. It can be any industry, any career field, any organization, other than teaching. How often do you think people have dipped into their own salaries to make things better for their coworkers or employees? I'd be willing to bet that it is not too often. Sure, people do things like bring donuts in for their coworkers, spending less than ten dollars each time. But what about purchasing things they need to get the job done? Most companies already provide the tools and equipment to perform work, and the employees don't necessarily have to spend out of their own pockets to get a task completed. Sometimes, maybe, but it is not the norm. It is very different for teachers, though. While managers and leaders in non-teaching organizations do not have to reach into their own pockets to further the work, teachers must do so. It is just the way it is, but it should not be this way.

You might be thinking that my idea is for nobody to go into their own pockets at all. On the contrary, I believe some should. While I do not agree with teachers having to do it, I believe that managers should. I believe that managers in non-teaching organizations should take a lesson from teachers everywhere, and spend their own money on their employees. It should be tempered for sure, based on their salaries and personal budgets. There are two things to think about here. First, a manager does not have to do this, whereas a teacher must. Secondly, a manager does not have to be a leader, whereas a teacher must. These are the differences.

If we spend out of our own pockets on our coworkers or employees when it is not required, we are displaying a sense of caring. We are displaying a sense of leadership, plain and simple. When the employee sees that we care, we are elevated in their eyes as someone who would go the extra mile for them. This is what leaders do. We take care of those we are charged with leading because it is the right thing to do. This thought references one of my favorite leadership quotes from two experts in the field, Warren Bennis and Peter Drucker. Each proclaimed, "Managers are people who do things right; leaders are people who do the right things." Taking care of our people is an example of doing the right thing, for sure. Dipping into our own pockets is an example of this.

A great example of this concept was demonstrated in the 1986 film, *Heartbreak Ridge*, directed by and starring Clint Eastwood as Gunnery Sergeant Thomas Highway. In the film, Gunny Highway is a hard-nosed U.S. Marine, charged with whipping a platoon of misfits into shape. At one point in the movie, a Marine from the platoon fails to show for the morning formation. When Highway asked why the Marine was not in formation, his platoon mates covered for him. But the Marine was absent without leave or AWOL, so Highway needed to investigate.

The scene shifted to later that evening when Gunny Highway arrived at the young Marine's home. Highway was met by the young man, his wife, and baby at the door. Thinking he was in hot water, the young man frantically tried to explain the reason for his being AWOL. He exclaimed that he had needed to take on another job to make ends meet. The family did not have enough money for rent, and it was something he was being forced to do. Just when things were looking bad for him, Gunny Highway did something that only a true leader would do.

He stuffed a wad of cash into the wife's hand so they could pay their rent. Shocked, the couple proclaimed their thanks. When asked why he made this gesture, Gunny replied, "Special fund, gunnery sergeants only." With that, he proceeded to step away, headed back to the Marine base. The scene ended with the young family embracing, ecstatic over the windfall, their money troubles temporarily abated.

Word of this got around, and the platoon quickly started on the road to recovery. It wasn't the fact that Gunny Highway gave some money to the Marine and his family, what mattered was that they now saw Gunnery Sergeant Thomas Highway in a different light. It had become apparent to them that he was a leader who cared for his people. He had been genuinely concerned for the Marine and his family, and it showed. He had finally earned the respect of every Marine in the platoon, thanks to that small gesture. After this occurred, they started following him and became more like the team they were supposed to be in the first place.

Yes, it was just a movie, but the message was very powerful. As leaders, we must care for our people. One of the ways to care for them is to know them and their plight and help however we can. Everyone has their personal challenges and we must be there for them if they need our help. I am not advocating that managers and leaders simply dish out money to fix everyone's problems. But what I am saying is that as managers and leaders, we should take a little bit of ourselves and show them that we care. Setting aside a little bit of money for this purpose is one of many ways of displaying this.

Managers and leaders should take a page from teachers' and coaches' lesson plans and playbooks. They should set aside funds for the betterment of the organization; it does not have to be much. Some companies allow for this but if not, the manager should do it anyway, and do his or her own small part. We can look at it from two different standpoints: from the manager, and the employee.

As a manager, using a special fund exclusively for their employees' benefit can be fulfilling for the manager. Think of it like this: a new employee comes on board, and the manager treats him to lunch while they discuss his new role. By ensuring the new employee is welcomed into the fold appropriately, the manager can feel confident that he has given the new employee a great opportunity to fit into his new work environment.

Managers should also set aside funds to show employees they care about their wellbeing. This can be anything from a personalized coffee mug to a team shirt to some other type of personal item. Unbelievably, some companies do not have it in their budgets to do these things for their employees. If this is so, then the managers should take it upon themselves. Making this type of effort also helps to elevate the culture of the organization. Yet again, doing this for a new employee will get them started on the right foot.

The possibilities are nearly endless, what a manager can do for his or her employees. Managers are there for them, and the organization becomes very healthy when this is done. Employees need to be told this; that the manager is there for them. When a manager embraces this thought and expresses it to the employees, they instantly start to become more of a leader instead of just a manager. Now for the employee's standpoint.

When a new employee is welcomed into an organization with a lunch or even a team shirt, he or she may more quickly meld into the organization. The new employee will have a sense that their new manager cares for their wellbeing, and thus, cares that they will get off to a positive start. When a new employee sees that the organization cares for him, he or she is more apt to not only fit in more quickly but also stay for a while.

They are on the road to becoming a happy, productive employee. As most businesses probably know, happy employees tend to do more quality work, which leads to better products or services. This, of course, leads to better company profits. So yes, employees enjoy receiving gifts as a welcoming package, but it should not stop there.

So, take that deep dive, why don't we? Meh, it can be a shallow one but we should still take it, nonetheless. Managers should maintain this fund and dive into it regularly. They should do this not only for newcomers but as an ongoing incentive program for the morale of the organization. The manager could bring in donuts, or cater a lunch for everyone. Again, the sky's the limit and should be budgeted appropriately.

But what about teachers and coaches? Well, yes, they should do it too. But notice my word choice: *should*. Teachers and coaches should not be forced into a deep dive to do their daily work. Rather, they *should* dive into their own funds if possible, and only if they desire to do so. For the most part, I think it would be agreeable to say that managers make more salary than teachers. So, it makes sense that a manager in a corporation is better positioned, money-wise, to set aside his or her own funds to that end. It is difficult for teachers and coaches to do this, so their hands should not be forced.

Whatever they do as managers and leaders in non-teaching organizations, they can all take a hint from teachers and coaches in this respect. Teachers and coaches love and care for their pupils and players. They demonstrate this, in part, by paying for stuff on their own. Do managers love and care for their employees? Sometimes. But remember, teachers and coaches do this because they must. Managers and leaders do this only if they want to.

When teachers, coaches, managers, and leaders dive deep into their own pockets, it shows they care. But what about the interactions between coworkers, regular employees? It is the same thing, but we don't always have to just spend money on people to show we care. We must interact and get to know each other to further our interpersonal relationships. This makes for healthy work culture when it gets right down to it.

When people get along with each other at work, productivity rises while bad feelings recede. We do this through healthy interaction with one another. Sometimes it is just conversation at the water cooler, and sometimes, it is a straight-up competition. One day, I purposely picked a fight with a coworker, simply because I wanted to see him operate in his environment. It wasn't a real fight, rather, A *Dogfight with Grover.*

A Dogfight with Grover

Fighter pilot is an attitude. It is cockiness. It is aggressiveness. It is self-confidence. It is a streak of rebelliousness, and it is competitiveness. But there's something else - there's a spark. There's a desire to be good. To do well; in the eyes of your peers, and in your own mind. — Robin Olds

I approached my co-worker's cubicle and said the words that most people would never dare to say to someone else in a professional work environment.

"I'll bet that I could kick your ass," I said with a wide grin.

"I beg your pardon?" he replied, his eyebrows raised inquisitively.

"In the sim. I'll bet that I can kick your ass in the sim."

"Oh, is that so?" he said with a wry smile and squinting eyes, the realization of what I was exclaiming dawning on him in an instant. "Okay, let's go."

Thus, began my lesson on why to never challenge an F-16 pilot to a duel. My coworker, 'Grover,' was a retired U.S. Air Force Lt. Colonel with more than 3,000 hours in the F-16 aircraft. Having retired from active duty, he was now my co-worker in the F-16 simulator facility, where he was a Contract Instructor Pilot or CIP. In this role, he provided training to fledgling U.S. Air Force student pilots as they learned how to employ the F-16 Fighting Falcon. My role was extremely different.

I had been a career aircraft maintainer in the U.S. Air Force (with only 4.3 hours as a passenger in an F-16) before retiring and becoming a Field Engineer, or 'Sim Tech.' As a Sim Tech, I performed maintenance and operation on the four F-16 flight simulators on site. I helped to support the training that Grover and the other CIPs delivered to the students daily.

One of my tasks as a Sim Tech was to perform what we called a 'preflight' on the simulators each morning. Not a preflight as one would think in the aircraft maintenance world, rather, we powered up the simulators and flew them to ensure that they were ready to go for that day's training sessions.

Usually, a preflight would consist of flying the sim for a little while to determine if the cockpit switches worked properly and the visual displays of the 'outside world' were not blurry or otherwise incorrect. Our facility had dozens of computers and projectors that were all required to work together for the simulator to be available for training. So, we took the preflight seriously…well maybe a little too serious. We looked for numerous things during our preflight, and the easiest way to conduct it was to load up a scenario where several computer-generated adversary aircraft would try to attack my co-workers and me as we flew in a loose formation. We reveled in shooting them out of the sky using our AIM-9 and AIM-120 missiles, and of course, the 20mm cannon. We also checked out the Radar Warning Receiver and the Chaff/Flare countermeasures systems before flying back to base and attempting landings. We evaluated the projectors along the way, ensuring they were providing the correct imagery. Doing it this way allowed us to get a good feeling that the simulator was going to work properly in all phases for the students that day. Doing a preflight in this manner was a little over the top, but it was our routine and we did it every morning for about an hour. Hey, it's a tough job but somebody has to do it, right?

Performing these preflights had left me with several dozen hours in the simulator, fighting against Flankers, Fulcrums, and other Sim Techs piloting their own simulated Vipers, so why not challenge a real fighter pilot to a duel? Piece of cake, right? Wrong! It was more like a mouse challenging a hawk to a duel. I checked the training schedule and found a free hour where we could connect two simulators for our dogfight. I scheduled the time for us and Grover and I agreed to meet up later.

We walked down to the mission control room and started getting our two simulator cockpits connected into an advanced, highly technical flight simulation. A flight simulator was comprised of one F-16 replica cockpit, which was inserted into its own 'dome' that displayed a simulated outside world to the pilot. This was done via twenty-two high-fidelity, two-thousand-pixel resolution projectors, splashing their video down onto the outside of the dome. We referred to it as a dome but in reality, it wasn't one. It was called a dodecahedron or 'dodec,' which is a series of flat pentagons arranged together so every side touched one another. It resembled a dome, but with flat screens instead of a smooth round surface. Once inside, the pilot can become immersed in the simulation and won't notice these flat screens or the seams that join them together. He or she is provided with a very accurate simulation of flying, albeit without the g-forces they become accustomed to during actual flight.

Once we had our two simulators connected and set into the simulation, we climbed into our cockpits and put on our communication headsets. Then, we 'ingressed' our cockpits into our domes via a long screw shaft that pulled the cockpit along a railroad track and into place inside the dome. We were in our domes, frozen in mid-flight while we got ourselves situated. I put my game face on and looked toward the front of the cockpit. Out in the distance in front of me was the rear end of another F-16, frozen in flight, awaiting the word to begin the simulation.

Another employee was manning the mission control console. He was responsible for taking the simulation out of 'freeze' so we could begin our fight and then resetting us back to the starting point once I shot my opponent down in flames. The simulation initialized our aircraft at eighteen thousand feet altitude and three hundred knots of airspeed. Once taken off of freeze, we would begin flying at those parameters.

"Okay, Mitch. This is the three-k BFM setup. I'm three thousand feet in front of you," said my opponent. He continued. "I'm *Viper One* and you are *Viper Two*. Are you ready?"

"Copy. Viper Two ready," I replied.

"Okay, Viper One, ready. Console, take us off of freeze." We began flying, his aircraft three thousand feet ahead of mine, flying level at eighteen thousand feet and three hundred knots.

"Viper One, ready," he said again after we were off of freeze.

"Viper Two, ready," I replied again.

"Viper, fight's on!"

I immediately flicked my left thumb outboard on the dogfight switch located on the throttle grip, which automatically locked my radar to his aircraft. My missile also acquired his engine exhaust heat signature, presenting me with the satisfying AIM-9 missile growl in my headsets. I moved my right thumb over to the weapons release switch, located on the sidestick controller. Just as I was getting ready to fire, he disappeared! His jet made a hard bank left and went immediately down. He also slowed down very rapidly as he descended below me and out of my sight. I tried to follow him by snapping my throttle to idle and banking left along with him. I pulled as hard as I could on the sidestick controller to make the jet turn around in chase.

Unfortunately, the energy my engine was producing made me extend way past the position he had just held in the sky. I couldn't match his turn, and he was gone, out of sight! Three seconds later and my dome flashed red as the simulated outside world flashed alternately red and sky, red and sky as my aircraft was simulated being destroyed by an AIM-9 missile.

"Viper One, FOX TWO! Kill F-16 left turn, fourteen thousand," Grover called out excitedly over his radio just as my dome began flashing red. "Vipers, knock it off. Viper One, knock it off."

"Viper Two, knock it off," I replied. The console operator hit the reset button and within a few seconds, we were back at the starting point with Viper One positioned directly in front of me. The entire dogfight lasted about six seconds. I was dead.

"Ready for another one, Mitch?" said Grover.

"Sure, I'll get you this time," was my reply.

"Okay, console, take us off of freeze." Our world started moving again.

"Viper One, ready."

"Viper Two, ready."

"Fight's on!" He quickly disappeared from my sight. I anticipated it this time, and had already moved to idle and deployed my speed brakes in an attempt to stay with him. This tactic didn't work either.

"Viper One, FOX TWO, kill F-16, left-hand turn, fifteen thousand," as my dome flashed red once again. Six seconds. "Vipers, knock it off. Viper One, knock it off."

"Viper Two, knock it off." The simulation reset once again.

"Okay, Mitch, let's try something different. We'll put you in front and see if you can get away from me." The console operator was following along, and after a quick flash of the visuals, I could not see any aircraft in front of me. I looked over my shoulder and there he was, three thousand feet behind me, waiting to shoot me down again.

"Console, take us off of freeze." We started flying. "Viper One, ready."

"Viper Two, ready."

"Fight's on!" I banked left and turned, just as I had seen him do on the last two engagements. I strained to look over my left shoulder and there he was, directly on my 'six.' I juked to the right and pulled hard on the sidestick. My aircraft banked back to the right and my airspeed slowed down tremendously, all of its energy depleted. I looked over my right shoulder and there he was, staring at me with his missiles and gun, toying with me. I saw a flash of smoke from his jet.

"Viper One, FOX TWO!" he announced over the radio. I banked my slow jet back to the left just as his AIM-9 made my dome start flashing red once again. "Vipers, knock it off. Viper One, knock it off."

"Viper Two, knock it off." The simulation reset again. "Grover, please tell me how to get away from you! I don't stand a chance like this!"

Grover laughed a little bit over the intercom, and then told me how to get away. "Okay, on 'fights on,' I want you to do this: first, chop the throttle to idle and go full boards. As you're doing that, roll one-hundred-twenty degrees of bank. When you're at one-twenty, pull as hard as you can. *If* I go by, then close the boards, go full AB and climb after me. It's as simple as that."

It's as simple as that. "Okay, I'll try it." I ran his instructions through my head again. "Okay, I'm ready."

"Console, take us off freeze. Viper One, ready."

"Viper Two, ready."

"Viper, fight's on!"

I executed the maneuver just as he instructed, pulling left with all my might. The simulated g-force on the heads-up display read '9G.' As I looked behind me, I could see his aircraft smoothly staying with mine. *He was supposed to fly right by!* Nope. I closed the speed brakes and put the throttle into military thrust, continued my turn, and popped out a flare. As I struggled to get away, fire came from his left wing root and I heard him very coolly say, "Viper One, tracking," as if he was ordering a cappuccino from a barista. His stating 'tracking' meant that his gunsight pipper was dancing all over the back of my aircraft, making figure eights from the back

106

of my canopy to the front of the tail. Luckily, I reacted quickly enough to defeat his gun kill attempt. I immediately pitched back to the right, punched it into afterburner, and pulled again. But he was right there, following me like a boat trailer. "Viper One, tracking…GUN KILL! F-16, right-hand turn, eleven thousand," Grover laughed over the radio. "Vipers, knock it off. Viper One, knock it off."

"Viper Two, knock it off." At least I had lasted a whole nine seconds on this one.

"You had enough, Mitch?" laughing again.

"Yeah I guess so, I'm out." I hit the button to egress from the dome, my cockpit rumbling backward on its tracks.

We climbed out of our simulators and met in the middle, both laughing at the dogfight we just had. Well, 'dogfight' probably wasn't the correct term for it. 'Ass-beating' is probably the better term, as Grover taught me a little bit about Basic Fighter Maneuvering or BFM during our little challenge. But it was all in good fun.

Grover and I had a great relationship over the years we worked together. We had been in the same fighter squadron for about a year, before our Air Force retirements, and worked together in the simulators for several years afterward. My statement that started all of this isn't usually something that co-workers would say to each other, ('I'll bet that I could kick your ass') without being reported to HR or being thumped on in the parking lot. But he and I worked very well together, and we had a very strong relationship. I'm grateful that he took the time out of his day to teach me how to 'die heroically,' but I also thought it was just pretty cool that I was able to spend some time with a great fighter pilot in his domain. I think that was my ultimate aim in making that statement to him.

Yeah, he schooled me alright. But it was a memorable experience for me, even though he beat me down, handily. I knew right from the start that he would destroy me, but I appreciated seeing him in his element and treating me like one of his students. Well, maybe not as a student, because he would have been a little more lenient on a student, I believe. He was just teaching me a lesson, so to speak, and not trying to have me learn the intricacies of employing the Viper in combat. It was simply a fun duel between two friends and colleagues.

Grover had left a lasting impression on me. Not because of our dogfight, rather because of his easy-going attitude and charisma. He was an expert in his field as an F-16 instructor pilot, and although he was easy going outside of the cockpit, inside it he was a fierce warrior. I think a lot of fighter pilots are like that, with differing attitudes inside versus outside the cockpit, their domain. We can correlate this to other types of professionals who are not fighter pilots, like teachers and coaches.

Teachers and coaches are absolutely the experts in their respective domains. I'm sure they are different outside of the classroom or playing field, but when they are in their element, they are all business. They take their jobs very seriously and care very deeply for their students and players. These professionals, these leaders in the middle, are worthy of our respect and adoration.

Yes, these professionals, these leaders, are worthy. Their personal sacrifices for their students and players are very evident, especially in this age of COVID. Teachers and coaches have had a difficult time of it, as you've read here. But, how could you relate to it, if the information came from an author like me? What you need to do is get it straight from the horse's mouth. Read about how these leaders in the middle have coped with COVID, how they have adjusted their leadership styles and teaching methods, thanks to all the changes they have been forced to endure. Saving the best for last, please enjoy the final chapter of the book, *Testimonials*.

Testimonials

It's the teacher that makes the difference, not the classroom. — Michael Morpurgo

This book has been an exercise in teachers and coaches leading from the middle, made by my experiences and lessons learned. But it is high time that we read about leadership directly from those who are in the middle, the teachers and coaches themselves, who have done so much for us. This time of COVID has been extremely difficult for everyone. But we all know that life goes on, that our children need to be educated, and sports need to be played. These leaders are instrumental in helping us to get back on our feet again.

This chapter is devoted to the people who enable this to happen, our leaders in the middle. For this chapter, I asked one question and received quite a bit of moving responses. As I read them, I sensed the leadership, emotion, and strength of these awesome individuals. I will step aside now, and invite you to read some real-world stories from the people affected the most: Teachers and Coaches.

~ ~ ~

Question:

How have you adapted your leadership style, and/or teaching or coaching methodology in response to the COVID-19 pandemic? How has it affected you, personally?

~ ~ ~

Samantha Hall

Teaching is a field that requires a leader who can provide a good example to the students. As a teacher, your response to situations determines the atmosphere of the classroom. In my five years of teaching, I have taught Title 1 students, who especially require more patience. A big part of being a teacher is being patient and trying to understand what your students are going through. As a Title 1 teacher, I am used to having students who are homeless, whose families are on food stamps, whose parents both may be working multiple jobs. Many of my students may be living with multiple generations in one household. Some of my students have neglectful parents, some had to be taken away from their parents. Some must work to help keep enough income in the household. Teachers who work in Title 1 often go through training in how to handle these situations. Even without the current pandemic, teaching students at a Title 1 school is often heartbreaking, and keeps you up at night. You as the leader must learn to pick your battles. You have to put yourself in your student's shoes and show compassion, as sometimes, you may be the only adult who shows them compassion at all.

When COVID-19 hit, struggles became even more difficult for students, especially those in Title 1 schools. I am a strict but fair teacher. I have always led my class with consistency and high expectations, while also being understanding. This year has forced me to take another step back and be even more understanding of my students. I know the traumas many of them face at home. I can't imagine how much worse this pandemic has made many of their lives. Some have lost family members; some have parents who lost their jobs. Many are helping babysit their younger siblings. This year, I have decided to be less strict than in previous years. I normally would not accept work weeks late, but this year I do. I have decided to focus on providing the support my students need to be successful in response to the shared trauma the world is experiencing.

I have chosen to continue showing compassion and helping my students find the resources they need to help with the depression and anxiety they are experiencing. I have had students fill out a check-in survey a few times to give them a place to vent and to let me know anything they want me to know. I can tell you, many of their stories have broken my heart. I learned to let things go, even when I did not want to. This year has been hard on me, and all teachers on an emotional level we have never experienced before. As teachers, we always think about our students and want to do what's best for them. I have had to learn to take care of myself first though, when in previous years that is not always something I have done.

Samantha Hall
Biology, Dysart High School
Dysart Unified School District
Surprise, AZ

~ ~ ~

Eric Godwin

First of all, the school in which I am employed has been in a one hundred percent virtual learning environment since we were sent home on March 13th, 2020. We started the 2020-2021 academic year virtually and I believe my school board and school division have done an outstanding job at supporting students, families, staff, and other employees during this pandemic.

I have personally adapted my leadership style to fit this virtual learning environment. One way I have done this is to ensure that I practice empathy with my students. This involves not trying to overstress my students and understanding that their home life may not be the best situation. This is why I do not pressure students to have their cameras on. They have learned to respect me more for this and I have seen students being more open to discussing various things with me due to maintaining a low-stress virtual classroom environment.

Another motto I have kind of adopted for my leadership style towards my classroom is "Redefine what success looks like." This is a quote from my book, *#ImpactMyLife: Being the Change*. I think this quote resonates with what is happening in today's classrooms. We have to internally adapt and understand that success might not be a letter grade or a completed assignment. Success in a virtual classroom may be a student who has gotten logged into Zoom on time for the first time that week or a student that has never had their camera on, but finally developed the courage to do so. Success in the classroom during the pandemic, in my opinion, is about growth, love, and opportunities. Allowing the students to grow through content and as individuals while simultaneously letting them know that you love them and you want them to be safe.

This pandemic has affected me personally. I have yet to lose a loved one from the pandemic, but it has reminded me how much I love the classroom. Being at home since March has not been the best. I miss the students in my classroom, in the hallway, and the cafeteria. Being able to connect with them in a way that I could never do in a virtual classroom. I have had moments of depression from just missing social connections from students and my peers that I work with. One of the reasons why individuals become teachers are because they are social butterflies and they love to talk which is one hundred percent me! When you take that away of course someone is going to feel down and unmotivated. Personally, I have joined a virtual book club and have talked on a couple of podcasts to be social again! I think this pandemic has affected people in multiple ways, but this is how it has personally affected me.

> Eric Godwin
> Science, Grace E. Metz Middle School
> Manassas City Public Schools
> Manassas, VA

$$\sim \sim \sim$$

Candi Tucker

Personally, I've struggled. I was at year twenty-three when we shut down. I had only weeks earlier applied for a regional support position for our state's education department and didn't get it. I would have been in a position to encourage and assist beginning teachers and recruit teachers to our rural and economically depressed area. I felt that if I were to make the professional jump out of the classroom into something higher it needed to happen then. When it didn't happen, I felt old, unaccomplished, and unnecessary.

I wasn't crushed because finally, after teaching thousands of students, *my child* was finally going to be at the school where I taught. I was going to rock the student activities for all of them, but also with a different lens coming from my own house. But the lack of activity and un-involvement through the Internet weighed on me.

I wasn't being the teacher I know I'm capable of and I wasn't able to support colleagues that I just finished my Master's for: no conferences to attend, limited face-to-face gatherings, difficult to simply fellowship with my coworkers. But over the winter break, I felt renewed. I contacted my principal who has supported and encouraged me with any crazy idea I've pitched and asked him to just say yes to whatever I've asked. He did.

In just the first week back, I've ordered birthday cards for the staff and since next Wednesday is Rubber Duckie day, there will be 100 random rubber duckies hidden around the campus. They can be redeemed for random prizes. I can't do all I want to do right now, but I can lift some spirits and perhaps boost that other teacher who is down in the dumps like I was last semester. As we work through this semester and plan for professional development and already work on programs next school year, I will be the staff's cheerleader.

Candi Tucker
Washington High School
Beaufort County Schools
Washington, NC

~ ~ ~

Alyson Pierce

In recent times it has made me reevaluate how I have been living, teaching, and coaching. Last year was my first year teaching and it is crazy to think I did not even get a full year of teaching under my belt before the education world as we know it changed. My in-person teaching strategy I developed was focused on first building relationships and then on teaching content. Since I am only a semester-based class (have my students half of the year) it is even harder to build connections with them due to the shorter time period. Pre-COVID I would attend students sporting events, concerts, tutor, and even helped coach some athletic teams to help my students see me in other than a teacher role. Building relationships was the key to getting my students to buy into their learning in my class. Many of my students come from struggling home lives and this can make it hard for them when they come to school. Therefore, I do not measure my student's success from merely passing my class or the state exam. I measure it on how much did I help them grow as a person and as a citizen.

In COVID times I am teaching all virtually, and this has been very difficult for my students because a large majority of them do not speak English. At the beginning of the school year, my first semester students struggled immensely with learning all of the different technology. They also struggled with keeping up with the course load for online classes. One way I have adapted from teaching from my first semester to my second semester online was creating example templates of the different projects to help students understand what they needed to do. I also helped demonstrate how to use a lot of the technology first, and now assume they know how to use it. By doing this, it helped save me a lot of time and headache.

I also found a virtual planner for students to use to keep track of all their work in their classes and map out how much time it would take them. Many of my students struggled the first semester with completing assignments and staying organized. The last thing I had to adjust this year was how I made connections with my students. This year since we were virtual has forced me to get even more involved in the school. I now host a virtual club for students to play virtual games, I am a part of the PBIS committee, have offered to be in several different videos, etc. This way my students can see me all over their virtual school day and get to know me. I often start class with a simple discussion about their lives and try to welcome them into getting to know my life.

The biggest thing I have learned from teaching is that students learn best when they form a bond with their teacher. This pandemic has made me realize to not take things for granted and forced me to adapt the ways I live my life. When I return to in-person learning I will do my best to not sweat the small things and try to dive deeper into learning more about my students' lives/cultures.

Alyson Pierce
Science, Grace E. Metz Middle School
Manassas City Public Schools
Manassas, VA

~ ~ ~

Ramon Bautista

The main issue that I have faced during this pandemic towards my teaching is really appreciating the fact that when we have students at school versus online. I have been at my school, with the support of my administration, and I have also been at home. I can honestly say that I have been in the trenches because I had tested positive and I know how it feels. When I was at school, I didn't have any students in my classroom and it was just me at my desk with all of the technology that I needed. My students would see me in my classroom and they would say, "I really miss being at school because you are able to understand the material much better." I totally agree with them. During this pandemic, I have never received so many emails and worked with technology like never before! With the support of my colleagues and my administration, they have inspired me to continue no matter what. Yes, this pandemic changed everything, and I mean everything that we used to do at school, we can no longer have or take advantage of.

I have a son who is a senior and what he has experienced as well, has put a damper with not attending activities, homecoming, and just even sharing experiences with his friends. Luckily, he did have a basketball season, and my wife and I were fortunate to celebrate his SENIOR NIGHT. My wife and I are both educators and one of the main things that we have faced is the hands-on and the lack of not having the appropriate materials that affect the student's academic performance. You can always talk to someone virtually but having that physical interaction is not the same. She is a librarian, and so it really has affected her and she misses having students going into the library for lessons and having discussions in person. When we have gone virtually, students are limited with the support. They are not supervised like if we were in the classroom, and so if I have students at home, some of them are really paying attention and taking notes. They are really focused and paying attention to what you are doing because they know better. You also have those that have their cameras off and you don't know what or if they are paying attention.

Ramon Bautista
Math, Hurshel Antwine Middle School
Socorro Independent School District
El Paso, TX

~ ~ ~

Scott Stemple

I have not altered my teaching philosophy in the slightest during the COVID-19 pandemic. My mode of instruction has certainly changed, but at its heart, my philosophy and focus remain the same. The child in front of me is what matters. Everything else is an abstraction, and in education, we live far too much in abstraction, in my opinion. We rely on data derived from the whole to determine our strategies for the individual. This is disrespectful of the individual, so I do everything in my power to personalize the educative experience of my students. That simply means the "shit" from above stops at me. It's labor-intensive, but it's the only way I can operate honestly within the system.

Scott Stemple

Lincoln Street Elementary School

Hillsboro School District

Hillsboro, OR

~ ~ ~

What an outstanding set of testimonials from the people who live it every day! We have read, first hand, how teachers and coaches have been forced to alter their leadership styles and teaching methods due to COVID. These exceptional professionals have demonstrated to us, as well as their students and players, that they have the expertise and drive that it takes to be leaders in the middle. They know how to lead their classes, their teams, and become beacons of light for their students and players to emulate and in some cases, revere. A hearty "Thank you" to all the professionals who participated and agreed to share their stories here. Now let's get to the *Conclusion.*

Conclusion

If you have to put someone on a pedestal, put teachers. They are society's heroes. — Guy Kawasaki

Well, this has been a fun book to write. It has been an honor to brag about teachers and coaches and what they do for their students and players every day. I began this venture with a singular story about Chuckie, and how he instructed the young lieutenant to succeed at aerial combat. As I wrote that story, I began to realize that there was much more to tell than one story about one teacher. I needed to do more.

Realizing the devastating effects that COVID-19 was having on our country, especially on education, I had an idea to do more. I felt that it was important to show the world, just how important our teachers and coaches were to us and our society. I needed to show that they were indeed leaders, and were leading from the middle of their organizations. Teachers and coaches were the heroes that students and players looked up to every day, whether it was in the classroom or over a Zoom conference. These terrific professionals have done real work for all of us, and I needed to show that because they deserved it.

So, I started to piece together different stories and lessons that I had either written previously or developed as I worked through the book. After Chuckie's story, I presented the chapter about football being leadership. Football is one of my passions, and I knew the players and coaches who were involved were leaders, so I felt their stories would fit here. Being a die-hard Seahawks fan, it was a little difficult for me to fawn over Tom Brady, but he deserved the praise for his legacy leadership. As I write this,

Tom Brady is celebrating winning his seventh Super Bowl in ten appearances, this time with the Tampa Bay Buccaneers. This is a legacy that will probably never be matched by anyone, ever. A seventh Super Bowl championship!

The next chapter about reluctant learners is something that every teacher is probably very familiar with. I felt it was very relevant here, as it takes a certain passion and strength to keep trying, and to get the information passed onto the student. This goes right along with the following chapter about taking a student one-on-one. Teachers and coaches often must speak privately with their students or player to ensure they learn the material. Maybe the student was reluctant, maybe it was something deeper. But it still needed to be done, because professional teachers and coaches don't let it slide. They are leaders, and as such, will find the underlying cause of a problem with their pupil. It's in their DNA as leaders. Sometimes, the student or player will come back years later to thank the teacher or coach for what they did.

I enjoy writing about leadership, and the next chapter describing the five leadership traits was a lot of fun for me. I felt that to be a successful teacher, one must have specific traits. This goes the same for those who are not in the teaching profession. While theirs might not align perfectly with the traits that I explained, each person will still come up with their reasons or traits on how they handle themselves in the classroom, or in a non-teaching organization for that matter.

The common theme as you read this part of the book was caring for people. The acronym GAS was all about caring. As leaders in the middle, we must Give A Shit about those we are charged with leading. This applies to teachers, coaches, and everyone else who works outside of those professions. We must care for people to be successful, to be happy. Caring is a basic tenet in leadership.

I went a bit deeper with this by explaining my thoughts on leadership theories and showing that everyone, especially teachers and coaches, can fall along a scale based on concern for people and concern for task. These four theories, transformational, transactional, servant, and laissez-faire, are paramount to learning about and then applying leadership. I believe everyone falls along that scale somewhere, no matter what profession they are in.

Speaking of going deeper, the next chapter discussed diving deep into our pockets to buy stuff for class. Every teacher alive knows how this is. It is a sad state that these professionals must dig into their own pockets to get their daily work done. This must be changed! It is not fair to force teachers to pay for their own supplies. There are two things to think about here. First, a manager does not have to do this, whereas a teacher must. Secondly, a manager does not have to be a leader, whereas a teacher must. These are the differences.

Next, I diverged away from leadership in the classroom to leadership in the workplace. I was happy to share my experience challenging a fighter pilot to a duel. This led to my demise, as I knew it would, but the reason I did it was to get to know Grover a little better and to strengthen our relationship. It just took a little bit of dying, is all. Healthy relationships are important in any professional setting. Of course, it is the same with teachers and coaches, even though I didn't write too much about them in that chapter. We're all leaders, regardless of our profession, and we can learn from each other by developing strong relationships with our coworkers.

The next, and last, chapter was my favorite, and I hope it was yours too. Receiving those testimonials from teachers and coaches who are living through this COVID experience was very moving for me. As I read each one, I marveled at their resilience and determination to get their jobs done, regardless of what COVID was doing to them and their students. These professionals were forced to alter their leadership styles and teaching methods in response to the pandemic, and their testimonials were the proof I needed to make it hit home. Getting it 'straight from the horse's mouth' was eye-opening, to say the least. Their stories ratified in my mind what I suspected all along, that these folks truly were leaders, plain and simple. I appreciated each of them for providing their comments and was humbled by their responses. I want to say "Thank you" to everyone who participated.

And now, I need to say this directly to all of you teachers and coaches out there. I want to say thank you again, but louder: **THANK YOU** to you professionals for what you do every day for your students and players, especially in this time of COVID and the difficulties that come with it. Understand that what you are doing for your students and players is not just for them. What you are doing for them, you are doing for each of us, our families, the country over, every day. Your leadership, perseverance, sacrifice, and dedication are why we are such a strong nation! It is because of you, that our children grow up and become successful in their own lives. It is because of you, that kids grow up and fondly remember their teachers and coaches. It is because of you, that these students and players emulate their leaders and become one themselves. It is because of **YOU**.

So, thank you. I'll leave you now with this quote:

If you can read this, thank a teacher. — Harry S. Truman

About the Author

Mitchell Boling is a Senior Field Engineer with a major Department of Defense contractor. In this role, he has been responsible for leading teams in the performance of operations and maintenance on F-16 and F-35 aircraft flight simulation training devices. During this period, he also went back to school and earned an MBA. He has been in this role since June 2008, after retiring from the U.S. Air Force as a Senior Master Sergeant.

Mitch joined the Air Force in July 1983 and began training as an aircraft maintainer, specifically learning the avionics systems on the F-16 *Fighting Falcon*. He worked in this same career field for the next twenty-five years and held numerous positions of greater responsibility and authority in the aircraft maintenance arena. He also traveled the world in the performance of his work, with numerous permanent and temporary duty assignments in various locations around the globe.

In 2003 he was assigned to Luke Air Force Base, Arizona, as a flight line production superintendent, and then the lead production superintendent. His last post in the Air Force was as the Luke Air Force Base wing avionics manager for the U.S. Air Force's largest fighter wing. In this demanding position, he reported directly to the maintenance group commander, the CEO of Luke's aircraft maintenance effort. His responsibilities included leading over 400 avionics personnel and overseeing avionics maintenance on more than 200 F-16 aircraft.

Mitch, an Air Force "Brat," was born in Berlin, Germany in 1963. Growing up, he moved around quite often with his family, eventually settling in Spokane, Washington. After joining the Air Force, he married his life-long love, the former Jodi Chamberlain of Hemet, California.

Having known each other since the age of seven and now happily married for over thirty-four years, they are blessed with two grown children and one grandson. Mitch and Jodi reside in Waddell, Arizona.

Other Books by the Author

Leadership: A View From the Middle offers a refreshing perspective from a leader in "the middle" of the workforce, down in the weeds with millions of other like-minded people. Part leadership lesson and part memoir, it presents true stories of the author's leadership experiences over two lengthy careers in the U.S. Air Force and afterward.

A career aircraft maintainer, Mitch Boling spent twenty-five years working on and sometimes flying in the F-16 Fighting Falcon. He uses these experiences to deliver leadership lessons that would be helpful to anyone seeking to navigate their way out of the middle and onto upper management and leadership positions.

This is an important contribution to the study of leadership. Whereas most books focus on the top of the organization, Boling shows how you can lead from wherever you are. As a veteran, I found his stories and lessons of leading others both in and out of the military to be real and relatable. He provides valuable insight on what it takes to lead effectively whether you are just starting out in your career or you are already a seasoned leader. --Jon S. Rennie, President & CEO, Peak Demand Inc.

Mitch recently published his first novel, *Persian Tomcats*. The year is 2003, and the United States is in the midst of its invasion of Iraq. Watching from across the border, The Islamic Republic of Iran is very interested in the activity. The Iranians see an opportunity to seize control of Iraq from the Americans and quell a centuries-long border dispute. They intend to conquer Iraq once and for all, but first, they must force out the Americans. To do so, they begin gearing up their F-14 "Persian Tomcat" fighters with a new weapon. Using these fighters, purchased from the U.S. decades earlier, will Iran find success? Not if the USAF 55th Fighter Squadron "Shooters" has anything to say about it.

While flying fighter jets is an exhilarating, dangerous profession, performing maintenance on them is difficult and sometimes overwhelming. Without the professionalism and dedication of the aircraft maintainers, the pilots would never be able to take to the skies. This story illustrates the special bonds that form between pilots and their maintainers, as one cannot perform their job without the other.

A story about piloting and maintaining the F-16 Viper, we join First Lieutenant Victoria "Shirley" MacMillan as she completes the USAF F-16 "Basic" course, becoming a full-fledged "Viper Driver." She is assigned to the Shooters at Shaw Air Force Base, where she meets Staff Sergeant Christopher Gray, an aircraft maintainer in the 55th Aircraft Maintenance Unit. The two of them play key roles in the conflict to come, attempting to stop Iran's Persian Tomcats.

Available on Amazon.

Made in the USA
Middletown, DE
21 August 2023

37089938R00076